BE
RESOLUTE
DETERMINING TO GO GOD'S DIRECTION

OT COMMENTARY
DANIEL

Warren W. Wiersbe

DAVID C COOK

transforming lives together

BE RESOLUTE
Published by David C Cook
4050 Lee Vance Drive
Colorado Springs, CO 80918 U.S.A.

Integrity Music Limited, a Division of David C Cook
Brighton, East Sussex BN1 2RE, England

The graphic circle C logo is a registered trademark of David C Cook.

—Unless otherwise noted, all Scripture quotations are taken from the King James Version of the Bible. (Public Domain.) Scripture quotations marked NASB are taken from the New American Standard Bible, © Copyright 1960, 1995 by The Lockman Foundation. Used by permission; NIV taken from the Holy Bible, New International Version®. NIV®. Copyright © 1973, 1978, 1984 International Bible Society. Used by permission of Zondervan. All rights reserved; NLT are taken from the Holy Bible, New Living Translation, copyright © 1996. Used by permission of Tyndale House Publishers, Inc., Wheaton, Illinois 60189. All rights reserved; and NKJV are taken from the New King James Version. Copyright © 1982 by Thomas Nelson, Inc.

Used by permission. All rights reserved.

Library of Congress Control Number 2008924755
ISBN 978-1-4347-6781-3
eISBN 978-1-4347-6589-5

© 2000 Warren W. Wiersbe

First edition of *Be Resolute* published by Victor Books°
in 2000 © Warren W. Wiersbe, ISBN 0-78143-305-3

The Team: Gudmund Lee, Amy Kiechlin, Jack Campbell, and Susan Vannaman
Cover Design: John Hamilton Design
Cover Photo: Veer Inc.

Printed in the United States of America
Second Edition 2008

15 16 17 18 19 20 21 22 23 24 25

030221

BE
RESOLUTE

CONTENTS

THE BIG IDEA

An Introduction to *Be Resolute*
by Ken Baugh

I've heard it said that there are two tests in life: the test of adversity and the test of prosperity. The challenge, of course, during the test of adversity is not to give in to despair, not to doubt God's love, power, and presence in our lives. The challenge during the test of prosperity is not to forget God, not to become self-sufficient and proud. I have discovered that my life seems to be in a constant state of flux between these two challenges.

For example, I believe that God is sovereign in my life, which simply means that nothing can happen to me that He does not allow for my good and His glory. I believe that God is a God of love, and as my loving Father I believe that God is always looking out for my best interests. I believe that God is with me all the time, that there is never a moment when I am alone. I believe these and the other attributes of God are true, and yet during times of adversity, I find my faith diluted by doubt. Sometimes I'm even tempted to despair. And then at other times in my life, when things are going good, I feel an ever-so-subtle shift in my heart away from depending on God, toward a sense of self-sufficiency. And then I wonder, *Why is it that God has my undivided attention during the times of adversity yet barely gets a nod from during the times of prosperity?* Can you relate to any of this? Is it possible to go through life without the major swings from doubt to self-sufficiency? Is it possible to be steady, stable, and resolute during these tests of adversity and prosperity? The answer is *YES!* Let me explain by using the life of Daniel as an example.

Daniel was a normal person just like us. He was tested by adversity and prosperity, yet he was able to remain resolute in his faith and relationship with God. Take the incident of the lions' den, for example. Prior to this incident, King Darius was thinking of making Daniel ruler over his entire kingdom due to his exceptional qualities and personal integrity. However, the other administrators and satraps were jealous of Daniel's favored position in the eyes of the King and sought to find something—anything in Daniel's life that they could use to discredit him. Yet, Daniel was such a man of godly character that according to 6:4–5 (NIV):

> They could find no corruption in him, because he was trustworthy and neither corrupt nor negligent. Finally these men said, "We will never find any basis for charges against this man Daniel unless it has something to do with the law of his God."

Daniel's character and work ethic were indisputable, and these deceitful men knew that the only way to hurt his credibility with the King would be to devise some type of trap that would force him into a moral dilemma with his God. Their plan was brilliant. They convinced King Darius to sign a law that required everyone in the land to worship him as God, and any who chose to rebel against this decree would be thrown into the lions' den. Knowing that Daniel would never bow down to anyone else but his God, these administrators and satraps thought they had devised the perfect plan to rid themselves of Daniel, and King Darius played right into their hands. Daniel quickly found himself in a moral dilemma. Should he continue with his daily prayer routine to the one true God, or should he submit to the decree of King Darius? Daniel knew the consequences that would ensue if he rebelled, but he stood firm in his convictions, and the Bible says that immediately after hearing of this decree Daniel went home to pray with the windows wide open so everyone could see (6:10). You gotta love that! Well, as the story goes, King Darius, bound by his own law, was required to throw Daniel into the den—the place where Daniel would face his greatest test of adversity.

The Bible doesn't tell us what was going through Daniel's mind during that long, dark night, but I sometimes wonder if he was tempted to doubt what he believed about God. Did he think to himself, *God, I have been faithful to you and now I find myself here in this forsaken place. God, I thought You loved me. God, I thought You would take care of me. What have I done to deserve this? Why me, God?* Well, we'll never know if Daniel struggled with doubt during this difficult time, but we can see from his answer to the king that his faith remained strong in the morning:

> At the first light of dawn, the king got up and hurried to the lions' den. When he came near the den, he called to Daniel in an anguished voice, "Daniel, servant of the living God, has your God, whom you serve continually, been able to rescue you from the lions?" Daniel answered, "O king, live forever! My God sent his angel, and he shut the mouths of the lions. They have not hurt me, because I was found innocent in his sight." (6:19–22 NIV)

Daniel passed the test of adversity with flying colors! After this incident, the Bible tells us that Daniel was raised to a position of prominence and prospered during the reign of both King Darius and Cyrus the Persian. As you read through the rest of the story about the life of Daniel, you will discover that he remained a humble, godly man of character throughout his years of prosperity as well.

The story of Daniel is a great example of a man who was able to navigate through the waters of both adversity and prosperity. But how did he do it? I believe that Daniel was able to stay resolute throughout the times of adversity and prosperity because his faith was anchored in the sovereignty of God. Daniel believed that God had everything in control, and that He was orchestrating all the events in the world around him to accomplish His purposes and to declare His glory. Here lies the big idea of the book of Daniel: God is sovereign over all things. I hope this book will give you a greater sense of confidence and hope in your own life as you navigate the tests of adversity and prosperity. Just remember that God has everything in control, and nothing can happen to you that He does not allow for your good and His glory.

***

Dr. Wiersbe's commentaries have been a source of guidance and strength to me over the many years that I have been a pastor. His unique style is not overly academic, but theologically sound. He explains the deep truths of Scripture in a way that everyone can understand and apply. Whether you're a Bible scholar or a brand-new believer in Christ, you will benefit, as I have, from Warren's insights. With your Bible in one hand and Dr. Wiersbe's commentary in the other, you will be able to accurately unpack the deep truths of God's Word and learn how to apply them to your life.

Drink deeply, my friend, of the truths of God's Word, for in them you will find Jesus Christ, and there is freedom, peace, assurance, and joy.

—Ken Baugh
Pastor of Coast Hills Community Church
Aliso Viejo, California

A WORD FROM THE AUTHOR

What Jesus said about the prophet John the Baptist, we could say about the prophet Daniel: "What did you go out into the wilderness to see? A reed shaken by the wind? But what did you go out to see? A prophet? Yes, I say to you, and more than a prophet" (Matt. 11:7, 9 NKJV).

Forced into circumstances that made it easy for him to become a reed in the wind, Daniel stood firm in the faith and dared to be different. Instead of bending and blending like a reed, he stood like a mighty oak, rooted in the Lord and defying the storms of change that raged about him.

Today's society is a good deal like the one Daniel lived in centuries ago. The world still wants God's people to conform to its standards and follow its practices. "Don't let the world around you squeeze you into its own mold" is the way J. B. Phillips translates Romans 12:2, and Daniel and his friends obeyed that admonition. We should obey it today. We need Christians who have the faith and courage to be resolute—not odd, but resolute.

As we study the book Daniel wrote for us, we'll meet Daniel's God, the Sovereign Lord who rules in the kingdom of men (4:32) and who confidently announces things to come. In Daniel's life and ministry we will see how true believers live in the light of biblical prophecy—how they relate to the Sovereign Lord and accomplish His good, acceptable, and perfect will.

In a world in which people find it easy to do what is right in their own eyes, the Lord is searching for men and women who will do what's right in His eyes and dare to be resolute. Will you be among them?

—Warren W. Wiersbe

A Suggested Timeline for Daniel

605 BC	Jerusalem taken by Nebuchadnezzar. Daniel and his three friends taken to Babylon.
602 BC	Daniel and his friends complete their three years of training. Nebuchadnezzar has his dream and Daniel explains it (Dan. 2).
586 BC	Jerusalem and the temple destroyed by the Babylonians.
539 BC	Belshazzar's feast (Dan. 5). Cyrus, king of Persia, conquers Babylon and reigns until 530.
538 BC	Cyrus decrees that the Jews can return to Judea and rebuild the temple.
537 BC	About 50,000 Jews return, led by Zerubbabel and Joshua the high priest. Daniel has his prophetic vision about the end times (10:1).
530–522 BC	Cambyses reigns. The rebuilding of the temple is stopped.
522–486 BC	Darius I reigns and the rebuilding is renewed in 520. The temple is completed and dedicated in 515.

THE CHRONOLOGICAL ORDER OF THE BOOK OF DANIEL

Chapters 1—4   Captivity and interpretation of dreams and visions.

Chapter 7   Vision of the four beasts.

Chapter 8   Vision of the ram and he-goat.

Chapter 5   Belshazzar's feast—conquest of Babylon.

Chapter 9   Vision of the seventy weeks.

Chapter 6   Daniel in the lions' den.

Chapters 10—12 Daniel's prayer and visions.

From 2:4 to 7:28, the book is written in Aramaic because the focus is on the Gentile nations. Daniel 1:1—2:3 and 8:1—12:13 are written in the Hebrew language.

A Suggested Outline of the Book of Daniel

Theme: God is sovereign in history
Key verses: Daniel 4:34–35

I. Daniel the Prisoner (Daniel 1:1–21)
II. Daniel the Interpreter (Daniel 2:1—6:28)
 A. Interpreting the image dream (Daniel 2)
 B. The golden image (Daniel absent) (Daniel 3)
 C. Interpreting the tree dream (Daniel 4)
 D. Interpreting the handwriting on the wall (Daniel 5)
 E. Daniel in the lions' den (Daniel 6)
III. Daniel the Seer (Daniel 7:1—12:13)
 A. The vision of the four beasts (Daniel 7)
 B. The vision of the ram and he-goat (Daniel 8)
 C. The seventy weeks appointed to Israel (Daniel 9)
 D. The vision of Israel's future and the end (Daniel 10—12)

Six different kingdoms are presented in this book: Babylon—the head of gold (2:32, 36–38) and the winged lion (7:4); Media-Persia—the arms and chest of silver (2:32, 39) and the bear (7:5); Greece—the thighs of brass (2:32, 39) and the leopard (7:6); Rome—the legs of iron (2:33, 40) and the "dreadful" beast (7:7); the kingdom of Antichrist—the ten toes (2:41–43) and the little horn (7:8); and the kingdom of Christ—the smiting stone that fills the earth (2:34–35, 44–45) and the Ancient of Days (7:9–14).

Chapter One

GOD RULES AND OVERRULES

(Daniel 1)

From May to September 1787, the American Constitutional Convention met in Philadelphia to develop a system of government for the new nation. By June 28, progress had been so slow that Benjamin Franklin stood and addressed George Washington, president of the convention. Among other things, he said: "I have lived, Sir, a long time, and the longer I live, the more convincing proofs I see of this truth—that God governs in the affairs of men."[1] He then moved that they invite some of the local clergy to come to the assembly to lead them in prayer for divine guidance. The motion would have passed except that the convention had no budget for paying visiting chaplains.

Though not a professed evangelical believer, Franklin was a man who believed in a God who is the Architect and Governor of the universe, a conviction that agrees with the testimony of Scripture. Abraham called God "the Judge of all the earth" (Gen. 18:25), and King Hezekiah prayed, "Thou art the God, even thou alone, of all the kingdoms of the earth" (2 Kings 19:15). In Daniel's day, King Nebuchadnezzar learned the hard way that "the Most High is sovereign over the kingdoms of men" (Dan. 4:32 NIV).

The first chapter of Daniel's book[2] gives ample evidence of the sovereign hand of God in the affairs of both nations and individuals.

GOD GAVE NEBUCHADNEZZAR VICTORY (1:1–2)[3]

For decades, the prophets had warned the rulers of Judah that their idolatry, immorality, and injustice toward the poor and needy would lead to the nation's ruin. The prophets saw the day coming when God would bring the Babylonian army to destroy Jerusalem and the temple and take the people captive to Babylon. A century before the fall of Jerusalem, the prophet Isaiah had proclaimed this message (Isa. 39), and Micah his contemporary shared the burden (Mic. 4:10). The prophet Habakkuk couldn't understand how Jehovah could use the godless Babylonians to chasten His own people (Hab. 1), and Jeremiah lived to see these prophecies, plus his own prophecies, all come true (Jer. 20; 25; 27). God would rather have His people living in shameful captivity in a pagan land than living like pagans in the Holy Land and disgracing His name.

The fall of Jerusalem looked like the triumph of the pagan gods over the true God of Israel. Nebuchadnezzar burned the temple of God and even took the sacred furnishings and put them into the temple of his own god in Babylon. Later, Belshazzar would use some of those holy vessels to praise his own gods at a pagan feast, and God would judge him (Dan. 5). No matter how you viewed the fall of Jerusalem, it looked like a victory for the idols; but it was actually a victory for the Lord! He kept His covenant with Israel and He fulfilled His promises. In fact, the same God who raised up the Babylonians to defeat Judah later raised up the Medes and Persians to conquer Babylon. The Lord also ordained that a pagan ruler decree that the Jews could return to their land and rebuild their temple. As missionary leader A. T. Pierson used to say, "History is His story."

God had made a covenant with the people of Israel, promising that He would care for them and bless them if they obeyed His statutes, but if they disobeyed, He would chasten them and scatter them among the Gentiles (Lev. 26; Deut. 27—30). He wanted Israel to be "a light to the Gentiles" (Isa. 42:6 NKJV) and reveal the glories of the true and living God; but instead, the Jews became like the Gentiles and worshipped their false gods. The nation's ungodly kings and civic leaders, the false prophets, and the faithless priests were the cause of the moral decay and the ultimate destruction of the nation (Lam. 4:13; Jer. 23:9–16; 2 Chron. 6:14–21). How strange that God's own people didn't obey Him, but Nebuchadnezzar and the pagan Babylonian army did obey Him!

So wise and powerful is our God that He can permit men and women to make personal choices and still accomplish His purposes in this world. When He isn't permitted to rule, He will overrule, but His will shall ultimately be done and His name glorified. We worship and serve a sovereign God who is never caught by surprise. No matter what our circumstances may be, we can always say with confidence, "Alleluia! ... The Lord God Omnipotent reigns!" (Rev. 19:6 NKJV).

GOD GAVE FAVOR TO DANIEL AND HIS FRIENDS (1:3–16)

The king's policy was to train the best people of the conquered nations to serve in his government. He could benefit from their knowledge of their own people and could also use their skills to strengthen his own administration. There were several deportations of Jews to Babylon both before and after the fall of Jerusalem, and it appears that Daniel and his three friends were taken in 605 when they were probably fifteen or sixteen years old. The prophet Ezekiel was sent to Babylon in 597, and in 586, the temple was destroyed.

A dedicated remnant (vv. 3–4a). Even a cursory reading of the Old Testament reveals that the majority of God's people have not always followed the Lord and kept His commandments. It has always been the "faithful remnant" within the Jewish nation that has come through the trials and judgments to maintain the divine covenant and make a new beginning. The prophet Isaiah named one of his sons "Shear-jashub," which means "a remnant shall return" (Isa. 7:3). The same principle applies to the church today, for not everybody who professes faith in Jesus Christ is truly a child of God (Matt. 7:21–23). In His messages to the seven churches of Asia Minor, our Lord always had a special word for "the overcomers," the faithful remnant in each congregation who sought to obey the Lord (Rev. 2:7, 11, 17, 24–28; 3:4–5, 12, 21). Daniel and his three friends were a part of the faithful Jewish remnant in Babylon, placed there by the Lord to accomplish His purposes.

These young men were superior in every way, "the brightest and the best," prepared by God for a strategic ministry far from home. They were handsome, healthy, intelligent, and talented.[4] They belonged to the tribe of Judah (Dan. 1:6) and were of royal birth (v. 3).[5] In every sense, they were the very best the Jews had to offer. Because Ashpenaz is called master of the eunuchs, some have concluded that the four Jewish boys were made eunuchs; but that is probably an erroneous conclusion. Originally, the term "eunuch" (Heb. *saris*) referred to a servant who had been castrated so he could serve the royal harem; but the title gradually came to be applied to any important court official. The word is applied to Potiphar and he was married (Gen. 37:36). The Jewish law forbade castration (Deut. 23:1), so it's difficult to believe that these four faithful Hebrew men who resisted Babylonian customs in every other way would have submitted to it.

A difficult trial (vv. 4b–7). It was an honor to be trained as officers in the king's palace, but it was also a trial; for these dedicated Jewish boys would have to adapt themselves to the ways and the thinking of the Babylonians. The purpose of the "course" was to transform Jews into

Babylonians, and this meant not only a new land, but also new names, new customs, new ideas, and a new language. For three years, their Babylonian teachers would attempt to "brainwash" the four Jewish young men and teach them how to think and live like Babylonians.

The name Daniel means "God is my judge," but it was changed to Belteshazzar or "Bel protect his life." Hananiah means "the Lord shows grace," but his new name, Shadrach, means "command of Aku" (the moon-god). Mishael means "Who is like God?" and the new name, Meshach, means "Who is as Aku is?" Azariah means "The Lord is my help," but "Abednego" means "Servant of Nebo (Nego)." The name of the true and living God was replaced by the names of the false gods of Babylon; but would we expect unbelievers to do anything else?

Learning a new language and even receiving new names didn't create much of a problem, but practicing customs contrary to the law of Moses was a great problem. The Babylonians were great builders, calculators, and military strategists, but their religion was steeped in superstition and myth. Just as Christian students in secular schools today often have to study material that contradicts what they believe, so Daniel and his friends had to master Babylonian history and science. In fact, in the final examination, they excelled all the other students (v. 20), and later, God gave them opportunities to show that their Jewish faith was superior to the faith of their captors. But when their course of training required them to disobey the holy law, they had to draw the line.

Surely the king's food was the best in the land, so why should these four Hebrew students refuse it? Because it would defile them and make them ceremonially unclean before their God (v. 8). It was important to the Jews that they eat only animals approved by God and prepared in such a way that the blood was drained from the flesh, for eating blood was strictly prohibited (Lev. 11; 17:10–16). But even more, the king's food would first be offered to idols, and no faithful Jew would eat such defiled food. The early church faced this same problem.

A discerning test (vv. 8–16). How can God's people resist the pressures that can "squeeze" them into conformity with the world? According to Romans 12:1–2, "conformers" are people whose lives are controlled by pressure from without, but "transformers" are people whose lives are controlled by power from within. Daniel and his three friends were transformers: Instead of being changed, they did the changing! God used them to transform the minds of powerful rulers and to bring great glory to His name in a pagan land.

The first step in solving their problem and being transformers was giving themselves wholly to the Lord. Daniel's heart—the totality of his being—belonged to the Lord, as did the hearts of his friends (Dan. 1:8; Rom. 12:1–2). "Keep your heart with all diligence, for out of it spring the issues of life" (Prov. 4:23 NKJV). A heart that loves the Lord, trusts the Lord, and therefore obeys the Lord has no difficulty making the right choices and trusting God to take care of the consequences. It has well been said that faith is not believing in spite of evidence—that's superstition—but obeying in spite of consequences. When they had to choose between God's Word and the king's food, they chose the Word of God (Ps. 119:103; Deut. 8:3).

The second step was to be gracious toward those in authority. The four men noticed that Ashpenaz was especially friendly and kind to them and recognized that this was the working of the Lord. (Joseph had a similar experience when he was in prison. See Gen. 39—40.) "When a man's ways please the LORD, He makes even his enemies to be at peace with him" (Prov. 16:7 NKJV). Instead of expecting a pagan Gentile officer to obey the law of Moses and get himself in trouble with the king, Daniel and his friends took a wise approach and asked for a ten-day experiment.

Throughout Scripture you will find courageous people who had to defy authority in order to obey God, and in every case, they took the wise and gentle approach. "If it is possible, as far as it depends on you, live at peace with everyone" (Rom. 12:18 NIV).

Along with Daniel and his friends, you have the examples of the Hebrew midwives (Ex. 1), the apostles (Acts 4), and even Jesus Himself (1 Peter 2:13–25). All of them had to resist the law in order to obey the Lord, and God gave them success. They were courteous and didn't try to get others into trouble. They had a meek and quiet spirit. They saw the challenge as an opportunity to prove God and glorify His name.

The four Jewish students didn't threaten anybody, stage a protest, or try to burn down a building. They simply excelled in their studies, acted like gentlemen, and asked Melzar to test them for ten days by feeding them only water and vegetables.⁶ Christians have no right to ask others—especially the unsaved—to take risks that they won't take themselves. Unconsciously directed by the Lord, Melzar was willing to accept their suggestion, and God did the rest. In the end, the four Jewish boys were healthier in body and better looking than all the other students. This is a vivid illustration of the promise in Matthew 6:33 and the principle laid down in Colossians 4:5; 1 Thessalonians 4:12; and 1 Peter 3:15.

When it comes to solving the problems of life, we must ask God for the courage to face the problem humbly and honestly, the wisdom to understand it, the strength to do what He tells us to do, and the faith to trust Him to do the rest. Our motive must be the glory of God and not finding a way of escape. The important question isn't "How can I get out of this?" but "What can I get out of this?" The Lord used this private test to prepare Daniel and his friends for the public tests they would face in years to come. The best thing about this experience wasn't that they were delivered from compromise, as wonderful as that was, but that they were developed in character. No wonder God called Daniel "greatly beloved" (Dan. 9:23; 10:11, 19), for he was very much like His Beloved Son.

GOD GAVE ABILITY AND SUCCESS TO DANIEL AND HIS FRIENDS (1:17–20)

If you want to make a living, you get training; and if you want to make a life, you add education. But if you want to have a ministry for God, you must have divine gifts and divine help. Training and education are very important, but they are not substitutes for the ability and wisdom that only God can give.

God's special blessing (v. 17). These four Hebrew youths had to study and apply themselves, but God gave them skill to learn the material, discernment to understand it, and wisdom to know how to apply it and relate it to God's truth. As students, all of us need to ask God for wisdom (James 1:5) and then work hard to do our very best. "Faith without works is dead" (2:26), and fervent prayer can never replace faithful study. Both are necessary.

What studies did these young men pursue? Surely they were taught the religion of Babylon as well as the system of astrology that formed the basis for both their religion and their science. The king's official counselors had to be able to interpret dreams and various omens, because understanding the times and knowing the future were both important to the king's success. The young men were given what we would call a "secular education" steeped in the superstition of that day.

But should the people of God learn "the wisdom of this world" when they have the inspired and infallible Word of God to instruct them? Some sincere believers think that all "worldly education" is sinful, while others, just as sincere, believe that God's people should understand the mind-set of the world but not be controlled by it. The great church father Tertullian

(160–220) is an example of the first group, for he asked, "What indeed has Athens to do with Jerusalem? What concord is there between the Academy and the church?"[7] He also wrote, "So, then, where is there any likeness between the Christian and the philosopher? Between the disciple of Greece and of heaven? Between the man whose object is fame, and whose object is life?"[8]

On the other hand, Moses was "learned in all the wisdom of the Egyptians" (Acts 7:22), and the apostle Paul read the classics and even quoted from them in his letters. In 1 Corinthians 15:33 he quoted the Greek poet Menander; in Acts 17:27 and 28, he quoted Epimenides, Aratus, and Cleanthes; and in Titus 1:12, he quoted Epimenides. In 2 Timothy 4:13, he asked Timothy to bring him his books and parchments, which were probably copies of some of the Old Testament Scriptures and possibly some of the classical writers. The point is that Paul knew the classics and sought to use what he knew to reach people with the truth of God's Word. "Beware of the atmosphere of the classics," Robert Murray M'Cheyne wrote in a letter to a friend. "True, we ought to know them; but only as chemists handle poison—to discover their qualities, not to infect their blood with them."[9]

By understanding the mind-set of the Babylonian people, especially the king's "magicians, enchanters, sorcerers and astrologers" (Dan. 2:2 NIV), Daniel and his three friends were better able to show them the superiority of God's wisdom. The Lord gave Daniel a special gift of understanding visions and dreams. In the first half of his book, Daniel interpreted the visions and dreams of others, but in the last half, he received visions of his own from the Lord.

The king's examination (vv. 18–20). We don't know how many students went through the entire course of study, but it's interesting that Nebuchadnezzar himself took the time to examine them. Since the new graduates were to become his personal advisers, the king wanted to be sure he was getting the best. By adding exceptionally intelligent new men to the staff, the king would be assured of getting the best counsel available. He was familiar with the older advisers and possibly not too happy with all of them (see 2:5–13). Was he suspicious of a palace intrigue? As we shall see later, the addition and the promotion of these four Jewish boys created jealousy and resentment among the advisers and they tried to get rid of Daniel (chap. 6). As older men, they resented their youth; as Babylonians, they resented their race; and as experienced servants, they envied their great ability and knowledge.

"Magicians" were men who dealt in the occult, while "enchanters" used incantations to accomplish their purposes. "Sorcerers" specialized in casting spells, "astrologers" studied the movements of the stars and their influence on events, and "diviners" sought to see the future by using various methods. Of course, all of these were forbidden by the law of Moses (Deut. 18:9–13). Daniel and his friends had to work alongside these men, yet they remained pure and gave a powerful testimony for the Lord.

The word *inquired* in Daniel 1:20 means "to examine and compare." The king not only questioned the graduates, but he also compared one with another, and in this way ended up with the very best. There's no reason why Christian students on secular campuses today shouldn't be among the finest students who win some of the highest awards to the glory of God. Tertullian didn't think that "Jerusalem" should have anything to do with "Athens," but if believers from "Jerusalem" don't witness to unbelievers in "Athens," how will these lost sinners ever hear about Jesus Christ? Going into "all the world" includes going to our pagan campuses and letting our lights shine.

GOD GAVE DANIEL A LONG LIFE AND MINISTRY (1:21)

The first year of King Cyrus's reign was 539 BC, but Daniel was still alive in 537 BC, the third year of Cyrus (10:1). If Daniel was fifteen years old in the year 605 when he was taken to Babylon, then he was born in 620, and he would have been eighty-three years old when he received the revelations recorded in chapters 10—12. While reading the prophecy of Jeremiah (25:11; 29:10), Daniel understood God's plan for the Jews to return to their land and rebuild the temple and the city (Dan. 9:1–2); and he lived long enough to see this prophecy fulfilled! How long he lived after that nobody knows, nor is it important that we know. During Daniel's long life, he had opportunity to witness to Nebuchadnezzar, Darius, Belshazzar, and Cyrus, as well as to the many court officers who came and went. He was a faithful servant, and he could say with the Lord Jesus, "I have glorified You on the earth. I have finished the work which You have given Me to do" (John 17:4 NKJV).

However, not every faithful servant of God is given the blessing of a long life. Stephen was probably a young man when he was martyred (Acts 7), and Paul was in his sixties when he was killed in Rome. The godly Scottish preacher Robert Murray M'Cheyne was two months short of being thirty years old when he died, yet his ministry still enriches us. William Whiting Borden ("Borden of Yale") was only twenty-five when he died in Egypt, and David Brainerd, missionary to the Native Americans, was only twenty-nine when God called him. "So teach us to number our days, that we may apply our hearts unto wisdom" (Ps. 90:12). We number our years, not our days, but everybody still has to live a day at a time, and we don't know when that final day will dawn.

In order to accomplish His plans for His people, the Lord providentially works to put some of His servants into places of special honor and responsibility. When He wanted to protect Jacob's family and the future of the nation of Israel, the Lord sent Joseph to Egypt and made him second ruler of the land. God had Esther and Mordecai in Persia, where they exposed a plot against the Jews and saved the people of Israel from being annihilated. Nehemiah was the king's cupbearer in Susa and was able to get royal assistance for restoring the walls of Jerusalem. I wonder if the men in high political office who assisted Paul were true believers in Jesus Christ (Acts 19:30–31; Rom. 16:23). Even if they weren't, God placed them where they were and enabled them to accomplish His will.

The events recorded in this chapter should be a great encouragement to us when we experience trials and testings and become discouraged; for when God is not allowed to rule, He overrules. God is still on the throne and will never leave us nor forsake us.

Has the enemy destroyed the holy city and the holy temple and taken God's people captive? Fear not, for there is still a godly remnant that worships the true God and serves Him. Does the enemy attempt to defile that godly remnant? Fear not, for the Lord will work on their behalf and keep them separated to Himself. Are godly believers needed in places of authority? Fear not, for the Lord will see to it that they are prepared and appointed. Does the Lord desire to communicate His prophetic truth to His people? Fear not, for He will keep His servants alive and alert until their work is done. Are you in a place of responsibility and wondering how long you can hold out? Fear not, for the same God who called you and equipped you is able to make you "continue" until you complete the tasks that He has assigned you. "He who calls you is faithful, who also will do it" (1 Thess. 5:24 NKJV).

Each believer is either a conformer or a transformer. We're either being squeezed into the world's mold or we're transforming things in the world into which God has put us. Transformers don't always have an easy life, but it's an exciting one, and it gives us great delight to know that God is using us to influence others.

QUESTIONS FOR PERSONAL REFLECTION OR GROUP DISCUSSION

1. In what ways, if any, do you think the process might have gone differently for the formation of our country had Benjamin Franklin been able to call in local clergy for prayer and dedication?

2. What does the fact of God's sovereignty mean to you in your everyday life?

3. Can you think of examples today where God uses people or powers outside of the church to cause Christians to turn back to Him?

4. List some people that you think of as the "faithful remnant" of Christianity in our world.

5. Daniel and his friends had to determine which parts of the Babylonian culture they could live with and which parts they should stand against. How do you make that determination in your own culture?

6. Describe a time when you or someone you know had to stand up for your beliefs as Daniel and his friends did in regard to the king's food.

7. What do you think enables a person to listen to the inner voice of God that tells him who he *is* above all the voices around telling him who he *should* be?

8. Name some of the challenges in confronting authorities without being unkind or angry.

9. In today's world, is it important to protest legislation that is contradictory to God's Word? What is the most effective way to do this?

10. How would you describe the traits that differentiate a "conformer" (someone who adjusts to the culture around him) from a "transformer" (someone who changes the world around him)?

Chapter Two

THE GOD OF DREAMS AND DESTINIES

(Daniel 2)

A s you turn from chapter 1 to chapter 2, the atmosphere in the king's palace changes radically. Chapter 1 closes with recognition and security, but chapter 2 introduces rejection and danger. Because they possessed almost unlimited power and authority, Oriental despots were notoriously temperamental and unpredictable, and here Nebuchadnezzar reveals this side of his character. (See also 3:19.) However, the hero and major actor in chapter 2 is not King Nebuchadnezzar but the Lord God who "reveals deep and secret things" (v. 22 NKJV). As you read this chapter, you witness the God of Israel in complete control of every situation and accomplishing His purposes even through superstitious Gentile unbelievers. Note the divine activities that protected His servants and brought glory to His name.

GOD DISTRESSES A KING (2:1)

Nebuchadnezzar was in the second year of his reign and discovering the burdens of the kingdom as well as the far-reaching consequences of his decisions. Some of his concerns were causing him restless nights (Eccl. 5:12), and his mind was unsettled as he worried about the future of his kingdom

(Dan. 2:29). How long would "Babylon the great" last? How long would he be the ruler? Shakespeare was right: "Uneasy lies the head that wears a crown."

The Lord gave Nebuchadnezzar a vivid dream that he couldn't understand, and it distressed him. That the Lord God Almighty would communicate truth to a pagan Gentile king is evidence of the grace of God. The phrase "dreamed dreams" may suggest that this one dream kept recurring. The Lord had given two dreams to Pharaoh (Gen. 41), another Gentile ruler, and Joseph had interpreted them; and He also gave a dream to the magi who came to worship Jesus (Matt. 2:12), and they were Gentiles. When God wanted to give a message to the Gentiles, He usually sent them a Jewish prophet (Amos 3:7)—Jonah to Nineveh, for example, or Amos to the neighboring nations (Amos 1—2). But here the Lord communicated directly to an unbelieving Gentile monarch. The Lord in His wisdom planned to use His faithful servant Daniel to describe and interpret the dream, and in this way, God's name would be glorified and Daniel and his friends would be honored and rewarded.

Does God still use dreams to communicate His will? Certainly He can do so if He pleases, but this isn't His usual approach. God guides His children today by His Holy Spirit as they pray, seek His face, meditate on His Word, and consult with their spiritual leaders. The danger is that our dreams may not come from the Lord. The human subconscious is capable of producing dreams, and Jeremiah 23:25–32 indicates that demonic forces can cause dreams that are Satan's lies and not God's truth. It's dangerous to accept dreams as messengers from the Lord.

GOD DISGRACES THE "WISE MEN" (2:2–13) [1]

The king did what any ancient ruler would do: He summoned his special advisers to help him understand the significance of this dream that had interrupted his sleep and robbed him of peace. But this was no routine meeting, for the king not only commanded them to interpret the dream but also to reveal the dream to him! If they didn't do both, he would kill them without mercy and turn their houses into public latrines and garbage dumps. This, of course, was a new challenge for them and they knew they couldn't meet it.

Here we are confronted with a question that sincere Bible students don't answer the same way: Did King Nebuchadnezzar forget his dream, or was he using this approach to test his counselors to see if they were authentic? I hold to the second position, but let's consider both sides of the matter.

He forgot the dream. I find it difficult to believe that such a vivid dream would pass out of the mind of a great leader like Nebuchadnezzar, particularly if the dream occurred more than once. Of course, we do forget most of our dreams, but in this case, the Lord was seeking to communicate His truth to the king. Surely the same God who gave the dream could see to it that the king would remember it. After all, the dream was so agitating that the king lay awake wondering what it meant. Furthermore, if indeed the king had forgotten the dream, how would he be able to verify it even if the advisers could come up with the right answer?

The KJV and the Amplified Bible translate verses 5 and 8 "the thing is gone from me," which can be interpreted "the dream has left me." This is probably the strongest argument for the king having a bad memory. But the NASB translates that same phrase "the command from me is firm," and the NIV translates it "this is what I have firmly decided." The reference isn't to the dream but to the king's edict of judgment. If the counselors couldn't tell him the dream and interpret it, they would be publicly humiliated and mercilessly slain.

The king was testing his counselors. I believe that Nebuchadnezzar remembered the dream, pondered it, and realized that it contained a significant message concerning him and his kingdom. It must have brought fear and wonder to his heart when he beheld this massive metallic image smashed to atoms by a mysterious stone that then grew into a mountain. The interpretation of this dream was too important for the king to treat it as a routine matter. He wanted to be sure that his "wise men" would give him the correct meaning, for his future was involved in that dream. He didn't want to hear "misleading and wicked things" (v. 9 NIV) that they made up just to please the king. He wanted the truth.

Perhaps he recalled the difference between the counselors he inherited from his father and the four Jewish young men who had graduated at the top of the class (1:19–20). He had seen that these four boys were ten times better than his counselors and possessed a wisdom far beyond anything the "wise men" had ever shown. Perhaps he had concluded that his "wise men" had conspired to deceive him and that their interpretations and explanations weren't valid at all. If indeed they had the ability to interpret the dream, then surely they also had the ability to tell him the dream! It was a test of their ability and their veracity.

Regardless of which approach is correct, this much is true: The counselors were greatly humiliated because they couldn't tell Nebuchadnezzar the dream. This was a great opportunity for them to receive wealth, prestige, and promotion, and the fact that they stalled for time indicated that they were unable to meet the challenge. This in itself set the stage for Daniel to exalt the true and living God of Israel who alone can predict the future (Isa. 41:21–23). By issuing this impossible challenge, the king was unconsciously following the plan of God and opening the way for Daniel to do what the counselors could not do. As they pleaded their case, the "wise men" tried flattery and logic, but all their speeches only made Nebuchadnezzar more and more angry, until finally he issued an edict that all the "wise men" in the city of Babylon be slain.

Throughout Bible history, you find occasions when God exposed the foolishness of the world and the deceptiveness of Satan. Moses and Aaron defeated the magicians of Pharaoh and the gods of Egypt (Ex. 7—12), and Elijah on Mount Carmel exposed the deception of Baal worship (1 Kings 18). Jeremiah confronted the false prophet Hananiah and revealed his wickedness (Jer. 28), and Paul exposed the deception of Bar Jesus the sorcerer (Acts 13:1–12). But it was Jesus who by His life, teaching, and sacrificial death declared the wisdom of this world "foolishness" with God, and that includes all its myths and false religions (1 Cor. 1:18ff.). The statement of the advisers in Daniel 2:10 wipes out astrology and other forms of human prophecy! Out of their own mouths they condemned their own practices!

GOD DISCLOSES THE SECRET (2:14–23)

The king's edict had to be obeyed, so Arioch, the captain of the king's guard and the chief executioner, set out to round up all the king's "wise men" and slay them. Satan had lost one battle, but now he would try to pull victory out of defeat by having Daniel and his three friends killed. The Evil One is willing to sacrifice all his false prophets in the city of Babylon if he can destroy four of God's faithful servants. Satan's servants are expendable, but the Lord cares for His people. See how the Lord intervened and accomplished His purposes and blessed His people.

Remarkable Postponement (vv. 14–16). When Arioch came to get Daniel and his friends, they were shocked to hear about the king's edict. As new "graduates" among the royal counselors, they hadn't been invited to the special session about the dream. Daniel spoke to Arioch "with wisdom and tact" (NIV), just as he had spoken to Ashpenaz and Melzar (1:9–14; see Col. 4:5–6), and the chief executioner explained how serious the matter was. By doing this and delaying his obedience, Arioch was risking his own life, but the officers in the palace had learned that the four Jewish men were trustworthy. Their gracious actions and words during their three years of training were now helping to save their lives.

Arioch allowed Daniel time to speak to Nebuchadnezzar, and the king must have been surprised to see him. Apparently his rage had subsided and he was willing to make some concessions. After all, Daniel hadn't been at the original meeting, so he deserved an opportunity to obey the king's orders. No doubt Nebuchadnezzar recalled that the four Hebrews had been exceptional students and were superior to the men whose lives were now in danger. Why kill your four best counselors just because of the incompetence of the others? By faith, Daniel promised to show the king his dream and the interpretation, for he knew that the Lord would answer prayer.

Believing prayer (vv. 17–19). Throughout this book, Daniel and his friends are presented as men of faith and prayer (Dan. 6; 9). They were far from home, but by faith they could "look toward" Jerusalem and the temple and claim the promise of 1 Kings 8:44–45. The God of heaven[2] would hear their prayers and answer them for His own glory. The word "secret" (*raz*) is used eight times in this chapter and is the equivalent of the Greek word *mysterion* ("mystery"), which is used twenty-eight times in the New Testament. It means "a hidden truth that is revealed only to the initiated." God had hidden prophetic truth in the dream and He enabled His servant to know both the dream and its interpretation and to understand God's future plans. "The effective, fervent prayer of a righteous man avails much" (James 5:16 NKJV).

Joyful praise (vv. 20–23). Daniel's first response was to bless the Lord for hearing and answering their petitions. They asked for wisdom, and God gave it (James 1:5), and His mighty hand stopped the execution process and gave the four men time to pray. Little did the pagan "wise men" realize that the presence of the Hebrews in Babylon was making their deliverance possible.[3] The God of heaven is also the God of history, for He can set and change the times allotted to rulers and to nations, which was the very thing Nebuchadnezzar was worrying about. The dream was "darkness" to the king but light to Daniel, not unlike the glory cloud that stood between Israel and the Egyptian army (Ex. 14:19–20). Daniel included his three friends in his song of praise (Dan. 2:23) because they had shared the burden of prayer with him. Later he would share the honors with them and they would serve with him in the highest appointed office in the city of Babylon.

When God's people today face a crisis, they need to follow the example of Daniel and his friends and take the matter to the Lord in prayer. Faith is living without scheming, and faith brings glory to God. Daniel and his friends couldn't take credit for what happened because it came from the hand of God. "Call upon Me in the day of trouble; I will deliver you, and you shall glorify Me" (Ps. 50:15 NKJV). "Whatever God can do faith can do," said A. W. Tozer, "and whatever faith can do prayer can do when it is offered in faith. An invitation to prayer is, therefore, an invitation to omnipotence, for prayer engages the Omnipotent God and brings Him into our human affairs."[4]

GOD DISPLAYS HIS WISDOM AND POWER (2:24–45)

Once again we see the wisdom and tact of Daniel as he went immediately to Arioch and told him not to destroy the "wise men" because God had revealed to him both the dream and its interpretation. Daniel never heard the Sermon on the Mount, but he knew how to treat his enemies and was willing to rescue the pagan advisers. Since Arioch was in charge of executions, he could stop the process and save the lives of all the king's counselors in the city of Babylon. Daniel gave Arioch the privilege of taking him into the presence of the king and sharing some of the credit. The statement, "I have found a man" (v. 25) isn't exactly the truth, because it was Daniel who found Arioch; but Daniel wasn't the kind of person who worried about who got the credit so long as God got the glory.

In reply to the king's question, Daniel immediately gave all the glory to the God of heaven, and in this he reminds us of Joseph when he interpreted Pharaoh's dreams (Gen. 41:16). Nebuchadnezzar must have been shocked when Daniel even told him that he knew the king had been worrying about the future of his kingdom before he had this dream. The dream was God's answer to his concerns, for God revealed the future sequence of the Gentiles' kingdoms and how Gentile history would climax with the appearance of an eternal kingdom.

The phrase "last days" ("latter days," "last times") is found frequently in Scripture, beginning with Genesis 49:1 and ending with 2 Peter 3:3. Our Lord ushered in the "last days" with His death, resurrection, and ascension to heaven (Heb. 1:2; 1 Peter 1:20), so we are living now in that period of time when God is "wrapping things up." God has plans for the "latter days" of Israel (Gen. 49:1; Deut. 31:29; Dan. 2:28), which will climax with Messiah returning to earth and being received by His people (Hos. 3:5; Mic. 4:1; Joel 2:28–29). The "last days" for the church include perilous times (2 Tim. 3:1), the apostasy of many, and the rise of scoffers and deniers of the truth (2 Peter 3:1ff.); and this period will end when Christ takes His church to heaven (1 Thess. 4:13–18).

The image Nebuchadnezzar beheld in his dream depicted what Jesus called "the times of the Gentiles" (Luke 21:24), a period of time that began in 605 BC when Jerusalem was taken by Nebuchadnezzar and the Babylonian army. This period will end when Christ returns to establish His kingdom (Luke 21:25–28).[5] During the "times of the Gentiles," there will be four successive kingdoms, climaxed by a fifth kingdom that will destroy the other four and fill the earth. The fifth kingdom is the kingdom of the Lord Jesus Christ, King of Kings and Lord of Lords.

The dream (vv. 31–35). First Daniel told the king what he had seen in his dream, and then he explained its meaning. He saw a large statue of a man, "an enormous dazzling statue, awesome in appearance" (v. 31 NIV), composed of five different materials: gold, silver, bronze, iron, and clay. Suddenly a stone appeared and smashed the feet of the statue so that the image was completely shattered and became like chaff that was blown away. Then the stone became a huge mountain that filled the earth. On hearing this accurate description, the king knew that Daniel was telling the truth and that what he said could be trusted. Only the God of heaven who sent the dream could have helped His servant know and interpret the dream.

The meaning of the dream (vv. 36–45).[6] The large image represented four Gentile kingdoms:

1. The head of gold—Nebuchadnezzar and the Babylonian kingdom (vv. 37–38). It lasted from 636 BC to 539 BC. Jeremiah called Babylon "a golden cup in the Lord's hand" (Jer. 51:7).

2. The breast and arms of silver—The Medo-Persian kingdom (539–330 BC). Darius the Mede conquered Babylon (Dan. 5:30–31).

3. The belly and thighs of bronze—The Grecian kingdom (330–63 BC). Alexander the Great established what was probably the largest empire in ancient times. He died in 323 BC.

4. The legs of iron and feet of iron and clay—The Roman Empire (63 BC–ca. AD 475). Iron represents strength but clay represents weakness. Rome was strong in law, organization, and military

might; but the empire included so many different peoples that this created weakness. "The people will be a mixture and will not remain united" (Dan. 2:43 NIV).

The destruction of the image represented the coming of Jesus Christ—the Stone—who would judge His enemies and establish His universal kingdom.

As simple as this explanation appears, it carries with it some important and profound messages. First, it reveals that God is in control of history. He knows the future because He plans the future. This doesn't mean that God is to blame for the evil things that leaders and nations do, but that He can overrule even their wickedness to accomplish His divine purposes. The God of heaven gave Nebuchadnezzar his throne and enabled him to defeat his enemies and expand his empire (vv. 37–38; Jer. 27). But the God who gave him his authority could also take it away, and He did (Jer. 50—51). The king didn't know how long his empire would last, but he knew it would end someday. In fact, Babylon was conquered by what Daniel called an "inferior" kingdom (Dan. 2:39).

Second, the dream reveals that human enterprises decline as time goes on. The massive and awesome image not only changed in value from head to foot—from gold to clay—but it also changed in strength, finally ending in feet made of iron mixed with clay. Actually, the statue was top-heavy, for the atomic weight of gold is ten times that of clay, and silver is five times heavier than clay. From age to age, nations and kingdoms appear strong and durable, but they're always in danger of falling over and crashing. The image Nebuchadnezzar saw dazzled him with the brilliance of the gold, iron, and bronze, but it was standing on feet composed of iron and clay.

As we survey history, on one level we see progress and improvement; but when we go deeper, we see decay and decline. Thoreau said that America had "improved means to unimproved ends," and that can be said of any developing nation. We can speak easily to people in almost any part of the world, but do we have anything important to say? We can travel rapidly from one place to another, but we make little progress in solving the problems of war, violence, famine, and liberty. While we're grateful for the things that make modern life comfortable and enjoyable—good houses, cars and planes, powerful medicines, electronic devices—we have to admit that each of these brings with it new problems that have to be solved. It's easier to make a living but harder to make a life.

A third truth is that it will be difficult for things to hold together at the end of the age. The feet of the image were composed of a mixture of iron and clay. Iron is strong and durable but clay is weak and prone to crumble. The iron in the image gives the appearance of strength and endurance, but the clay announces just the opposite. In fact, the clay robs the iron of its ability to hold things together, for wherever the iron touches the clay, at those points there is weakness. Society today is held together by treaties that can be broken, promises that can be ignored, traditions that can be forgotten, organizations that can be disbanded, and money-making enterprises that can fail—all of it iron mixed with clay!

Man at his best is clay, for God made him out of the dust of the earth. Though man and woman are both made in the image of God, sin has robbed us of the dominion He gave us (Gen. 1:26). We are both creators and destroyers, and we seem bent on destroying one another and the world God has graciously given us. The heart of every problem is the problem in the human heart—rebellion against God.

The image gives us a fourth truth: Jesus Christ will return, destroy His enemies, and establish His kingdom. The stone is a frequent image of God in Scripture and especially of Messiah, Jesus Christ the Son of God (Ps. 118:22; Isa. 8:14; 28:16; Matt. 21:44; Acts 4:11; 1 Cor. 10:4; 1 Peter 2:4–8). The phrase "without hands" is used in Scripture to mean "not by human power" and refers to something only God can do (Col. 2:11; Heb. 9:11, 24). It appears that the Roman Empire will in some ways continue until the end of the age and culminate in the rule of ten kings (Dan. 2:44; 7:24–27; Rev. 17:3, 12–18). The world will be delivered from evil, not by a process, but by a crisis, the promised return of Jesus Christ. Whatever remains of the four Gentile kingdoms, passed from one kingdom to the next, will be destroyed and turned into chaff. Then Christ will establish His kingdom, which will fill all the earth.

When we consider these truths, our response ought to be one of joyful confidence, knowing that the Lord has everything under control and will one day reign on this earth. While God's people should do everything they can to alleviate suffering and make this a safer and happier world, our hope is not in laws, political alliances, or moral crusades. Our hope is in the Lord. People's hearts need to be changed by the grace of God, and that means God's people must be witnesses to the ends of the earth. The only kingdom that will stand forever is Christ's kingdom (Dan. 2:44), and the only people who will be citizens of that kingdom are those who have trusted Him and been born again by the Spirit of God (John 3:1–18).

What would all of this have meant to King Nebuchadnezzar as he sat on his throne listening to a young Jewish lad explain God's mysteries? For one thing, the message of the image should have humbled him. It was not Nebuchadnezzar who conquered nations and kingdoms; it was God who enabled him to do it and who gave him his empire. "You, O king, are a king of kings," said Daniel. "For the God of heaven has given you a kingdom, power, strength, and glory" (Dan. 2:37 NKJV). Alas, the great king forgot this lesson and one day said, "Is not this great Babylon, that I have built for a royal dwelling by my mighty power and for the honor of my majesty?" (4:30 NKJV). God had to humble the king and make him live like an animal until he learned that God does according to His will (v. 35) and alone deserves glory.

In giving the dream and enabling Daniel to know the dream and explain it, God displayed His wisdom and power. God has the wisdom to plan the ages and the power to execute His plan. King Nebuchadnezzar ruled from 605 BC to 562 BC, but Jesus Christ will reign forever and ever, and of His kingdom there shall be no end.

GOD DISTINGUISHES HIS SERVANTS (2:46–49)

Being a pagan unbeliever, Nebuchadnezzar was so overwhelmed by what Daniel did that he treated him as though he were a god! Cornelius the Roman centurion treated Peter that way (Acts 10:25–26), and Paul and Barnabas were accepted as gods by the people of Lystra (14:8–18). Being a devout Jew, Daniel must have abhorred all this adulation, but he knew it was useless to protest the commands of the king. But in paying homage to Daniel, the king was actually acknowledging that the God of the Hebrews was greater than all other gods. Nebuchadnezzar hadn't yet come to the place where he believed in one true and living God, but this was the first step.

What the king did and said also announced to everyone in the court that Daniel was superior to the Babylonian advisers who could not describe the dream, let alone explain it. And yet what Daniel and his friends did saved the lives of those men!

The king kept his word and promoted Daniel with great honors, just as Pharaoh honored and promoted Joseph in Egypt (Gen. 41:39–43). He made Daniel ruler over the province of Babylon and, at Daniel's request, made his three friends helpers with him in that office. They were put in different offices in the province, while Daniel remained at the court of the king and sat in the king's gate, a place of great authority (Dan. 2:49 NIV). What started out as possible tragedy—the slaughter of four godly men—was turned into great triumph; and the God of Daniel received great glory.

QUESTIONS FOR PERSONAL REFLECTION
OR GROUP DISCUSSION

1. Why don't we expect God to speak to us through dreams today as He
   did during Daniel's day?

   God still speaks through dreams,
   Scripture gives us his message

2. What kinds of magic, myths, and mysticism compete with God's Word
   now, as the magicians competed with Daniel in King Nebuchadnezzar's court?

   The media

3. Prayer sustained Daniel and his friends while they were exiled in
   Babylon. In what ways has prayer sustained you when you were in a
   difficult time?

   Many times – daily

4. What keeps us at times from remembering to praise God for answers
   to our prayers, as Daniel did?

   We do not take time

5. Wiersbe says, "Faith is living without scheming." How do you agree or
   disagree with that statement?

   Faith is trusting

6. If Daniel were sitting here, what reasons do you think he would give for saving the lives of the king's counselors?

Counselors are souls

7. What does it mean to you that "God is in control of history"?

I know all things are working together for good

8. How do we become a part of God's efforts in the world so that we are doing His bidding wherever we are? *Where ever we can find a job encouraging othe*

9. Who are the people today who have the opportunity to influence our world's leadership the way Daniel influenced the king?

Every Christian

10. How can we best pray for the people in our world who have opportunities like Daniel to bring glory to God?

Pray for oorselves -

Chapter Three

FAITH AND THE FIERY TRIAL
(Daniel 3)

The Devil tempts us to destroy our faith, but God tests us to develop our faith, because a faith that can't be tested can't be trusted. False faith withers in times of trial, but true faith takes deeper root, grows, and brings glory to God. This explains why God permitted the three Hebrew men to be tested and then thrown into the fiery furnace. The apostle Peter must have been well acquainted with the book of Daniel because he used the metaphor of the "fiery trial" when he warned his readers of the persecutions about to come to the church (1 Peter 1:7; 4:12).[1]

The experience of these three men helps us examine our own faith and determine whether we have the kind of authentic faith that can be tested and bring glory to God.

TRUE FAITH CONFRONTS THE CHALLENGE (3:1–12)

We don't know how much time elapsed between the night Nebuchadnezzar dreamed about the metallic image (Dan. 2) and the day he commanded the people to fall down before the golden image that he had made. Some students believe that the event described in Daniel 3 might have occurred twenty years after the promotion of Daniel and his friends, about the time Jerusalem was finally destroyed (586 BC).

The heart of the king (vv. 1–3). When Daniel explained the meaning of the successive metals in the massive image, he identified Nebuchadnezzar as the head of gold (2:38), and perhaps this is what helped motivate the king to make an image of gold. Not content to be merely a head of gold, he and his kingdom would be symbolized by an entire image of gold! There was definitely an element of pride in this whole enterprise. Daniel had made it clear that no empire would last, including that of the great Nebuchadnezzar. The king's heart was filled with pride because of all his conquests, but along with that pride were fear and concern for himself and his vast kingdom. He wanted to make sure that his people were loyal to him and that there would be no rebellions.

There wasn't enough gold in his entire kingdom to make a solid image ninety feet high and nine feet wide, so the image was probably made of wood overlaid with gold (Isa. 40:19; 41:7; Jer. 10:3–9). But it must have been an awesome sight to see this golden image standing on the plain at Dura, a location perhaps six miles from the city of Babylon. ("Dura" simply means "a walled-in place," and there were several sites with that name in ancient Babylon.) Also in the area was a furnace into which people would be thrown if they refused to fall down before the image and acknowledge the sovereignty of King Nebuchadnezzar. Nebuchadnezzar planned to unify his kingdom by means of religion and fear. The alternatives were to fall down before the image and worship or be thrown into the furnace and be burned to death.

The king sent official messengers to all the provinces of his empire, commanding the officials to gather for the dedication of the great golden image. Eight different officers are especially named (Dan. 3:2–3) and they would represent the people left back home. Princes (satraps perhaps) were the chief administrative officers in the provinces, while governors were probably their assistants (or perhaps military commanders). Captains ruled over the smaller districts in the provinces, and judges were their advisers. Treasurers served as do treasurers today, and counselors were experts in the law. Sheriffs were local judges and magistrates, and rulers were the miscellaneous officials in the province. Every level of authority was represented and all were expected to be present.

But this was more than a political assembly; it was a religious service, complete with music, and it called for total commitment on the part of the worshippers.[2] Note that the word *worship* is used at least eleven times in the chapter. Nebuchadnezzar was wise to use instrumental music because it could stir the people's emotions and make it easy for him to manipulate them and win their submission and obedience. Throughout history, music and song have played an important role in strengthening nationalism, motivating conquest, and inspiring people to act. Music has the power so to grip human thoughts and emotions that people are transformed from being free agents into becoming mere puppets. The English poet William Congreve wrote that "music has charms to soothe a savage breast," but music also has power to release the savage in the breast. Music can be used as a wonderful tool and treasure from the Lord or as a destructive weapon from Satan.

The hearts of the people (vv. 4–7). The herald didn't ask for a vote. He simply told the people that what was about to happen was a matter of life or death. At the sound of the music, they would either fall down before the image or they would die. But the superstitious crowd was accustomed to worshipping many gods and goddesses, so the command was an easy one to obey, especially in light of the consequences. The difference between the true believer and the unbeliever isn't the presence of faith, because everybody lives by faith in something. The difference is in the object of that faith. The crowd believed the herald and the king, and therefore they obeyed.

The three Hebrew men believed the commandment of God, so they disobeyed. The crowd had credulous faith, but the Jews had confident faith.

"Faith is one of the forces by which men live," said philosopher and psychologist William James, and he was right. People act by faith when they step into an elevator, order food in a restaurant, drive on the highway, or say their marriage vows. The Christian believer lives by faith in the living God and what He has revealed in His Word. The great multitude of Babylonians, exiles, and representatives from the provinces simply conformed to the edict of the king and did what everybody else was doing. "After all," they argued, "we all have to live!" There were thousands of Jewish exiles in Babylon, and they were represented by Shadrach, Meshach, and Abednego. If they bowed to the idol, all the Jews were involved!

This assembly of "worshippers" helps us better understand the plight of people in today's world who don't know our Lord Jesus Christ. They blindly follow the crowd and build their lives on the false and the futile. Concerned only with survival, they'll do almost anything to escape danger and death, even to the point of selling themselves into slavery to men and the empty myths that they promote. It's the philosophy of the Devil: "Skin for skin! Yes, all that a man has he will give for his life" (Job 2:4 NKJV). It's quite the opposite of the outlook of the Christian believer who believes John 12:24–26.

The hearts of the three Jewish men (vv. 8–12). But there were three men in that great crowd who stood tall when everybody else bowed low. Their faith was in the true and living God and in the word that He had spoken to their people. Knowing the history of the Jewish people, they were confident that the Lord was in control and they had nothing to fear. The prophet Isaiah had written, "Fear not, for I have redeemed you; I have called you by your name; you are Mine. When you pass through the waters, I will be with you; and through the rivers, they shall not overflow you. When you walk through the fire, you shall not be burned, nor shall the flame scorch you" (Isa. 43:1–2 NKJV). Faith means obeying God regardless of the feelings within us, the circumstances around us, or the consequences before us.

It's difficult to reconstruct the logistics of the event, but it seems that King Nebuchadnezzar and his advisers ("Chaldeans") were not together as they watched the event and that the king didn't require them to join with the crowd in their worship. They may have affirmed their loyalty privately and it would be an insult for them to join with "the rabble" in their worship. Since the three Hebrew men held offices in the province (Dan. 2:49), they had to be there; but we don't know where they were standing.[3] Apparently Nebuchadnezzar couldn't see them but the Chaldeans could; in fact, these evil men were no doubt watching and waiting for the opportunity to accuse these foreigners who had been promoted over the heads of the Babylonians. We don't know that this was the same group of advisers who was embarrassed when Daniel interpreted the king's dream, but if so, they quickly forgot that these "foreigners" had saved their lives.

True faith isn't frightened by threats, impressed by crowds, or swayed by superstitious ceremonies. True faith obeys the Lord and trusts Him to work out the consequences. These three Jewish men knew the law of God— "You shall have no other gods before Me.... You shall not bow down to them nor serve them" (Ex. 20:3, 5 NKJV). Once the Lord has spoken on a matter, the matter is settled and there's no room for discussion or need for compromise. To bow before the image even once, no matter what excuse they might give, would have destroyed their witness and broken their fellowship with God. The tense of the Greek verb in Matthew 4:9 indicates that Satan asked Jesus to worship him only one time, and the Savior refused. Shadrach, Meshach, and Abednego would not bow down to the golden image even once because it would lead to serving Nebuchadnezzar's false gods for the rest of their lives.

TRUE FAITH CONFESSES THE LORD (3:13–18)

Once again we see the king in a fit of anger (v. 13; see v. 19; 2:12). He had conquered many cities and nations, but he could not conquer himself. "Better a patient man than a warrior, a man who controls his temper than one who takes a city" (Prov. 16:32 NIV). Yet the three Hebrew officers were calm and respectful. "Always be ready to give a defense to everyone who asks you a reason for the hope that is in you, with meekness and fear" (1 Peter 3:15 NKJV).

The king must have had special respect for these men and the work they did in the empire because he gave them another opportunity to comply with his orders. He may have forgotten that he had called their God "the God of gods, the Lord of kings" (Dan. 2:47 NKJV), because he arrogantly asked, "And who is that God that shall deliver you out of my hands?" (3:15; and see Ex. 5:2). He was actually claiming to be a god himself! In a short time he would be humbled and have to confess that the God of the Hebrews is "the Most High God" and that nobody should blaspheme His name.

The three men could have compromised with the king and defended their disobedience by arguing, "Everybody else is doing it," or "Our office demands that we obey," or "We'll bow our knees but we won't bow our hearts." They might have said, "We can do our people more good by being officers in the king's service than by being ashes in the king's furnace." But true faith doesn't look for loopholes; it simply obeys God and knows that He will do what is best. Faith rests on commands and promises, not on arguments and explanations.

Times of adversity are usually times of opportunity, especially when God's people are being persecuted for their faith. "You will be brought before rulers and kings for My sake, for a testimony to them" (Mark 13:9 NKJV). The three courageous Jews weren't concerned about themselves, nor were they afraid of the fury of the king. Their only concern was obeying the Lord and giving a faithful witness to all who were watching and listening. Their attitude was respectful and their words were few and carefully chosen.

"We are not careful to answer" (Dan. 3:16) means, "We don't need to defend ourselves or our God, for our God will defend both Himself and us." They weren't the least bit worried! It's a bit arrogant for God's people to think they have to defend God, for God is perfectly capable of defending Himself and taking care of His people. Our task is to obey God and trust Him, and He will do the rest. "Behold, God is my salvation; I will trust, and not be afraid: for the Lord Jehovah is my strength and my song; he also is become my salvation" (Isa. 12:2).

Shadrach, Meshach, and Abednego were men of faith but not men of presumption. Had they affirmed that God would deliver them, that would have been presumption, because they didn't know what God had willed for their situation. Instead, they stated that their God was able to deliver them, but even if He didn't, they still wouldn't fall down before the king's golden image. There is such a thing as "commercial faith" that says, "We will obey God if He rewards us for doing it." Again, it's the Devil's philosophy of worship: "All these things I will give You if You will fall down and worship me" (Matt. 4:9 NKJV; Job 1:9–12). In my pastoral ministry, I've heard people make promises to God so they can "persuade" Him to heal them or change their circumstances. But this isn't believing in God—it's bargaining with God. True faith confesses the Lord and obeys Him regardless of the consequences. From the very beginning of their time in Babylon, Daniel and his three friends determined that they would be different, and the Lord enabled them to maintain that determination.

Hebrews 11 lists the names and deeds of great men and women of faith, including these three Jewish men (Heb. 11:34), but at verse 36, the writer says "And others" and then lists people who seem to be failures in spite of their faith (vv. 36–40). The Greek word means "others of a different kind," that is, others who had faith but didn't see God do the miracles He did for those listed in the first thirty-five verses. God always rewards faith, but He doesn't always step in and perform special miracles. Not everybody who prays is healed, but God always gives strength to bear with pain and grace to face death without fear. The three Hebrew men believed that God could deliver them, but they would trust Him even if He didn't. That is how faith is supposed to operate in our lives. (See Hab. 3:17–19.)

TRUE FAITH CONFOUNDS THE ENEMY (3:19–25)

The king's temper once more got the best of him—proud men don't like to be disobeyed—and he ordered the three Jewish believers to be thrown into the fiery furnace. They had turned down his generous offer, so they had to suffer the consequences. Whereas before, the king had been friendly with them and concerned to save them, now he was determined to destroy them. At last the court advisers would get their revenge on these Jewish exiles who had encroached on their territory and been promoted to the offices that belonged to the Chaldeans.

The furnace was used for smelting ore. It had a large opening at the top through which fuel and vessels full of ore could be placed into the fire, and there was a door at the bottom through which the metal was taken out. An opening in a wall enabled the smelters to check on the progress of their work, and through holes in the wall they could use bellows to make the fire blaze even more. The unit was large enough for at least four persons to walk around in it. It was into this furnace that Nebuchadnezzar cast the three faithful Jews, fully clothed and bound. It seemed like certain death for the men who refused to obey the king.

The king's anger must have affected his mind, for the best way to punish the men wasn't to increase the temperature but to decrease it. A hotter fire would kill them instantly and then burn them up, but a lower temperature would cause them to suffer intense pain before they died. However, it made no difference because the men weren't affected by the fire at all! When the king looked into the furnace, he saw that they were alive and not dead, loose and not bound, and that there was a fourth person with them! The king thought it was an angel who looked like "a son of the gods" (vv. 25, 28 NIV), but the fourth person in the furnace was Jesus Christ in one of His preincarnate appearances in the Old Testament (Isa. 43:2; Ps. 91:9–12). They were walking about as though they were in a palace and not in a furnace! The ropes with which the three men had been bound were the only things that had been affected by the fire. The God of Shadrach, Meshach, and Abednego was indeed able to deliver them!

The three men had refused to obey the king's order to fall down before the image, but when the king ordered them to come out of the furnace, they immediately obeyed. They were living miracles, and they wanted everybody to know what their great God could do. Not only was each man's body whole and the hair unsinged, but their clothing didn't even smell like fire. The other officials at the dedication service witnessed this marvel (Dan. 3:27) and no doubt reported it when they arrived back home. What a story! The officers wouldn't dare speak up at that time, lest they offend their king. But King Nebuchadnezzar spoke out (v. 28)! He affirmed (1) the power of the God of Israel, (2) the effectiveness of faith in Him, and (3) the remarkable dedication of the three Jewish men who gave their bodies to the true God and not to the king's false god (Rom. 12:1–2). By one act of faith, the three Jewish men became witnesses of the true and living God to the entire Babylonian Empire!

TRUE FAITH CONFIRMS THE PROMISES (3:26–30)
Why did the Lord include this story in the Old Testament Scriptures? For

the same reason He included stories about the "faith experiences" of Abraham, Moses, Joshua, David, and the prophets: to encourage God's people in their battle against the world, the flesh, and the Devil. "For whatever things were written before were written for our learning, that we through the patience and comfort of the Scriptures might have hope" (Rom. 15:4 NKJV).

Encouragement in Daniel's day. Things couldn't have been worse for the Jewish people than they were during the period of the seventy years captivity in Babylon. Their land was devastated, the temple and the city of Jerusalem were in ruins, and the people were either scattered among the Gentiles or in bondage in Babylon. The situation looked hopeless. The prophets foresaw the day when the Jews would return to their land and rebuild the city and the temple, but first they had to endure the shame and suffering of captivity.

The experience of Shadrach, Meshach, and Abednego must have greatly encouraged the faithful Jews and brought conviction to the Jews who were compromising with the enemy. These three men sent a strong message to their people: Jehovah God is still on the throne, He hasn't forsaken us, and He will one day fulfill His promises to His people. He promised to be with them in their furnace of affliction if they would trust Him and obey His will. Later, when the remnant returned to the land, the account of the fiery furnace must have helped to sustain them in those years of difficulty and delay.

Encouragement in our day. Life may be fairly safe and comfortable where you and I live, but in many parts of the world, God's people are paying a high price to maintain their testimony and their separation from the world. Day after day, they hear the herald shouting, "Fall down before the golden image! Everybody is doing it!" In his first epistle, Peter warned the church that the "fiery trial" was about to begin, and surely they remembered what happened to the three Hebrew men in the days of Nebuchadnezzar. We are told that there were more martyrs for Christ during the twentieth century than during all the preceding centuries. Not all believers have been spared death in the furnace, but they have been spared compromising their witness for Christ and taking the easy way out. "Be faithful until death, and I will give you the crown of life" (Rev. 2:10 NKJV).

As we move toward the end of the age, the furnace of opposition will be heated seven times hotter, and the pressure to conform will become stronger and stronger. It will take a great deal of grace, prayer, courage, and faith for God's people to stand tall for Christ while others are bowing the knee to the gods of this world. The book of Daniel is a great source of encouragement, because it reminds us that God cares for His people and honors them when they are true to Him. "Them that honour me I will honour" (1 Sam. 2:30).

Encouragement for the future. The events in Daniel 3 remind us of prophecies found in the book of the Revelation, especially chapters 13 and 14. There will one day arise a world leader like Nebuchadnezzar ("the Beast") who will have an image of himself constructed[4] and will force all the people of the world to worship him. The people who obey will be given a special mark on their forehead or their hand, and this mark will be the passport for staying alive and doing business. Those who refuse to obey will be persecuted and many of them slain (Rev. 13:4, 7, 12, 15). But the Lord will seal to Himself 144,000 Jews whom the Beast will not be able to touch, and they will come through the tribulation time to reign in Messiah's kingdom.

As our studies progress, we shall see that Daniel's book has a special bearing on "the time of the end" (Dan. 12:4) and that his prophecies will enlighten and encourage believers living in those difficult last days (Matt. 24:15). No matter how despotic the world's rulers become or how hot they stoke the furnace, God will be with His people in the furnace and will ultimately defeat their enemies and establish His kingdom.

> When through fiery trials thy pathway shall lie,
> My grace all sufficient shall be thy supply;
> The flame shall not hurt thee; I only design
> Thy dross to consume and thy gold to refine.
>
> —AUTHOR UNKNOWN

QUESTIONS FOR PERSONAL REFLECTION
OR GROUP DISCUSSION

1. What kinds of things does the Devil do to destroy our faith?

   The Devil seeks to get us to faith in the words of God

2. Think about the examples of true faith that you have witnessed. How would you describe the characteristics of true faith?

   True faith is believing in the promises of God

3. The king used music to get the people to worship the idol. In what ways is music used today to build our allegiances to something or someone?

4. What do you think made the difference between the Jews who fell down and worshipped the idol and the three who didn't?

   The Crowd had credulous faith but the Jews had confident faith

5. List some ways we are asked to compromise within our culture if we are going to fit in with the general public.

6. What kinds of concerns distract us from being concerned with what God wants from us?

7. How do you think it would feel to make a choice of faith that you knew could very easily result in your own death?

Tough

8. If you had been one of the many Jews who had worshipped the idol, how do you think the experience of these three men would have affected you?

I would have been embarrash,

9. As we get closer to the end of the world, what kinds of compromises do you think we will face as a people of faith?

How we worship

10. How would you define the kind of faith that gives you the strength to not conform?

Trusting

Chapter Four

LEARNING THE
HARD WAY
(Daniel 4)

This is a unique chapter in the Bible because it's an official auto-biographical document, prepared by the king of Babylon and distributed throughout his vast kingdom.[1] That Nebuchadnezzar should openly admit his pride, his temporary insanity, and his beastly behavior, and then give glory to the God of Israel for his recovery, is indeed a remarkable thing. He learned an important lesson the hard way just as people are learning it the hard way today: "Pride goes before destruction, and a haughty spirit before a fall" (Prov. 16:18 NKJV).

There are five "acts" in this extraordinary drama.

1. AGITATION: THE KING'S DREAM (4:4–18)[2]

Some students believe that twenty or thirty years may have elapsed between the episode of the fiery furnace described in chapter 3 and the events described in this chapter. Nebuchadnezzar was now enjoying a time of peace and security. After defeating all his enemies and completing several impressive building projects, he was able at last to rest at home and delight in what had been accomplished. Nebuchadnezzar thought that he was the builder of "Babylon the great" and the architect of its peace and prosperity, but he was soon to learn that all these things had been permitted by the will of the Most High God.

Once again God in His grace used a dream to communicate an important message to Nebuchadnezzar. In his first dream (Dan. 2), the king saw a great metallic image of which he was the head of gold, but in this dream he saw a huge flourishing[3] tree that fed and sheltered a host of animals and birds. He heard an angel command that the tree be chopped down, its branches and leaves cut off, its fruit scattered, and its stump banded with iron and bronze. Then a command from the angel announced that someone would live like a beast for "seven times" and then be restored. After the first dream—that of the great image—King Nebuchadnezzar was troubled (2:3), but after this second dream, he was terrified (4:5 NIV). He summoned his wise men and asked them for the interpretation of the dream, but they were baffled; so he called for Daniel. After the experience of the first dream, when the wise men failed so miserably, you would think Nebuchadnezzar would have bypassed his advisers and called Daniel immediately. But it seems that in the record of both of these dreams, Daniel is kept apart from the wise men, even though he was "master of the magicians" (v. 9). The Lord wants to remind us that the wisdom of this world is futile and that only He can give a true understanding of the future.

Nebuchadnezzar had changed Daniel's name to Belteshazzar, which means "Bel protect his life" (vv. 8, 19; see 1:7). Bel (Marduk) was one of the king's favorite gods. The fact that Nebuchadnezzar used both the Hebrew name and the new name in this document suggests that he had grown fond of Daniel over the years and didn't treat him like the ordinary exile. The king recognized that "the spirit of the gods" was in Daniel and had given him remarkable wisdom and insight.[4]

The king described his dream to Daniel: the vastness of the tree (note the repetition of "all" in vv. 11–12), the terrifying words of the angel, the transformation of a man into a beast, and the affirmation of the angel that all of this was by the decree of the Most High God. The dream was sent to teach an important lesson: "The Most High is sovereign over the kingdoms of men and gives them to anyone he wishes and sets over them the lowliest of men" (v. 17 NIV). God saw the pride in Nebuchadnezzar's heart and was prepared to deal with it. The king could issue his decrees (2:13, 15; 3:10, 29; 6:7–10, 12–13, 15, 26), but it was the decrees from the throne of heaven that ruled events on earth (4:17, 24; 9:24–27). "The LORD has established his throne in heaven, and his kingdom rules over all" (Ps. 103:19 NIV).

2. INTERPRETATION: THE KING'S DANGER (4:19–26)

After hearing the description of the dream, Daniel was stunned and troubled, and the king could see the perplexity on his face.[5] Daniel's thoughts were troubled because he saw what lay ahead of the successful monarch. He tactfully prepared the king for bad news by saying that he wished the dream applied to the king's enemies and not to the king. (See 2 Sam. 18:32.) We get the impression that Daniel had a great personal concern for the monarch, and as they had worked together in the affairs of Babylon, he had sought to introduce him to the true and living God.

Years before, Daniel had announced to Nebuchadnezzar, "You are this head of gold" (Dan. 2:38 NKJV); and now he announced, "It [the tree] is you, O king" (4:22 NKJV). Trees are often used in Scripture as symbols of political authority, such as kings, nations, and empires (Ezek. 17; 31; Hos. 14; Zech. 11:1–2; Luke 23:31). With the help of the Most High and by His decree, Nebuchadnezzar had built a vast empire that sheltered many nations and peoples. He ruled a great kingdom, a strong kingdom, and a kingdom whose dominion reached "to the end of the earth" (Dan. 4:22).

But the king was taking credit for these achievements and was in great danger because his heart was becoming proud. The king had learned from the first dream that the Most High God ruled in the kingdom of men and no earthly throne was secure. The Babylonian kingdom would end one day and God would raise up another kingdom to take its place. In the episode of the fiery furnace, Nebuchadnezzar had witnessed the miracle of the preservation of the three faithful Hebrew men, and he had decreed that nobody speak against their great God (3:29). But now Nebuchadnezzar was about to meet this Most High God and receive severe discipline from His hand.

The cutting down and trimming of the tree symbolized Nebuchadnezzar's disgrace and removal from the throne, but the leaving of the stump was a promise that he would one day reign again.[6] The banding of the stump may suggest that he was marked by God and protected by Him until His purposes for him were fulfilled. For seven years ("seven times") the king would live like a beast, eating grass and feeling the forces of nature against his body. Years later, Daniel would tell Nebuchadnezzar's grandson Belshazzar that his grandfather had lived with the wild donkeys (5:21).[7]

The grand lesson God wanted the king to learn—and that we must learn today—is that God alone is sovereign and will not permit mortals to usurp His throne or take credit for His works. We are but creatures, and God is the Creator; we are only subjects, but He is the King of Kings. When men and women refuse to submit themselves to God as creatures made in His image, they are in grave danger of descending to the level of animals. It's worth noting that God used animals when He wanted to describe the great empires of history (Dan. 7), and that the last great world dictator is called "the beast" (Rev. 11:7; 13:1ff.; 14:9, 11; etc.).

Men and women are made in the image of God, but when they leave God out of their lives and resist His will, they can descend to the level of animals. "Do not be like the horse or like the mule," warned King David, who was guilty of acting like both (Ps. 32:9 NKJV). Like the impulsive horse, he rushed into sin when he committed adultery with Bathsheba, and then like the stubborn mule, he delayed confessing his sins and repenting (2 Sam. 11—12). When the Lord arrested Saul of Tarsus on the Damascus Road, He compared the pious rabbi to a stubborn ox when He said, "It is hard for you to kick against the goads" (Acts 9:5 NKJV).

3. EXHORTATION: THE KING'S DECISION (4:27)

Daniel concluded his explanation of prophecy with an exhortation to obedience and urged the king to turn from his sins and humble himself before the Lord (v. 27). Unlike some preachers, Daniel didn't divorce truth from responsibility. There was a "therefore" in his message. I have participated in numerous prophetic conferences and heard a great deal of interpretation and some speculation, but I haven't always heard personal and practical application. Some of the speakers talked a great deal about what God would do in the future, but they said very little about what He expected of His people in the present. An understanding of God's plan imposes on the hearer the responsibility to do God's will. To hear and understand the Word but not obey it is to deceive ourselves into thinking we have grown spiritually when we have actually moved backward (James 1:22–27).

"We can speak so glibly about the coming of our Lord and about the judgment seat of Christ," said William Culbertson, late president of Moody Bible Institute. "You do not truly hold the truth of the doctrine of the return of the Lord Jesus Christ until that doctrine holds you and influences your manner of living as the Bible says it should."[8] Peter's admonition in 2 Peter 3:11–18 explains how Christians behave when they really believe the Lord will return.

In ancient times, an Eastern monarch exercised supreme authority and was master of life and death. Daniel knew that the king had a violent temper (Dan. 2:12; 3:19) and that he was walking a dangerous path as he confronted him with his sins; and yet the faithful prophet must proclaim the Word and leave the consequences with the Lord. Moses learned that in the court of Pharaoh, and so did Nathan in the court of David when he told the king "You are the man!" (2 Sam. 12:7 NKJV). Elijah boldly confronted wicked King Ahab and Queen Jezebel (1 Kings 18:17ff.), Isaiah rebuked Hezekiah (Isa. 39), and John the Baptist told King Herod to break off his evil relationship with Herodias (Mark 6:14–29). Preachers who tailor their messages to please people will never enjoy the blessing of God.

Unlike the Jewish rulers, who were supposed to be accessible to their people and serve them as shepherds, Eastern kings lived in splendid isolation and heard only the good news. Being a high official in the land, Daniel knew that Nebuchadnezzar had not been concerned about the poor or shown mercy to those in need. Daniel also knew how many times in the law of Moses the Lord spoke of Himself as the protector and defender of the poor, the aliens, and the oppressed. Perhaps Nebuchadnezzar had exploited the people in pursuing his extensive building operations, and wealth that should have helped the poor had been used to gratify the selfish appetites of the proud king. "If a king judges the poor with fairness, his throne will always be secure" (Prov. 29:14 NIV), but Nebuchadnezzar was about to lose his throne.

Daniel was calling for repentance. He wanted the king to change his mind, acknowledge his sins, turn from them, and put his faith in the true and living God, the Most High God of the Hebrews. Nebuchadnezzar knew enough about Daniel's God to know that what Daniel spoke was the truth, but he did nothing about it.[9] The king was passing up a gracious opportunity to make a new beginning and submit to the will of the Most High God. He made the wrong decision.

4. HUMILIATION: THE KING'S DISCIPLINE (4:28–33)

"All this came upon the king Nebuchadnezzar" (v. 28), because God's Word never fails to fulfill its purposes.[10] God graciously gave the king an entire year in which to heed His warning and repent of his sins, but the king refused to yield. Pride had so gripped his heart that he would not submit to the Most High God. "Because the sentence against an evil work is not executed speedily, therefore the heart of the sons of men is fully set in them to do evil" (Eccl. 8:11 NKJV). God waited patiently in the days of Noah and gave the inhabitants of the world 120 years to turn from their sins, but they refused (1 Peter 3:20; Gen. 6:3). He gave the city of Jerusalem almost forty years of grace after the religious leaders crucified their Messiah, and then the Romans came and destroyed the city and the temple. Just think of how longsuffering He has been with this present evil world (2 Peter 3:9)!

Nebuchadnezzar was probably walking on the flat roof of his palace, looking out over the great city when he spoke those fateful words recorded in Daniel 4:30.[11] One thing is sure: He was walking in pride (v. 37), and pride is one of the sins that God hates (Prov. 6:16ff.). "When pride comes, then comes shame; but with the humble is wisdom" (11:2 NKJV). "God resists the proud, but gives grace to the humble" (James 4:6 NKJV; Prov. 3:34; 1 Peter 5:5). It was pride that transformed the angel Lucifer into the Devil (Isa. 14:12–15), and it was pride that brought about the downfall of King Uzziah (2 Chron. 26:16–21).

A solemn voice from heaven interrupted the king's egotistical meditations and announced that the time of probation had ended and judgment was about to fall. We never know when God's voice will speak or His hand touch our lives. Whether it's the call of Moses in Midian (Ex. 3), the drafting of Gideon to lead the army (Judg. 6), the opportunity of David to kill a giant (1 Sam. 17), the summons to the four fishermen to leave all and follow Christ (Matt. 4:18–22), or the warning that life has come to an end

(Luke 12:16–21), God has every right to break into our lives and speak to us. What the king had learned from Daniel's interpretation of the dream, he now heard from heaven! "No man knows when his hour will come" (Eccl. 9:12 NIV).

God is longsuffering with sinners, but when the time comes for Him to act, there is no delay. The words were still on Nebuchadnezzar's lips when everything began to change. His heart became like that of an animal (Dan. 4:16), and he was driven from the royal palace to live in the fields with the beasts. Since the man was beastly at heart, God allowed his brutish nature to be revealed openly. It's likely that Daniel and the other officers managed the affairs of the kingdom during the king's seven years of discipline, so that when the king returned to the throne, he found everything in good order. That in itself was a strong witness to Nebuchadnezzar of God's grace and Daniel's faithfulness. How much the common people knew about this judgment isn't revealed in the record. It's been suggested that the court officials kept the king in the palace gardens and not in the public eye, but Daniel 5:21 states that he was driven from people and lived with wild donkeys. His mind and heart, and even his body, became beastly for seven years.[12]

God could have destroyed both the king and his kingdom, but He still had purposes to fulfill for His people and His prophet Daniel. Furthermore, God wanted the king to tell the whole empire what He had done for him so that His name would be glorified among the nations. It was the privilege and responsibility of Israel to be a light to the Gentiles (Isa. 42:6; 49:6), but they failed miserably and started practicing the darkness of the pagan nations. So God used a pagan king to give glory to His name!

5. RESTORATION: THE KING'S DELIVERANCE (4:34–37, 1–3)

The first-person narrative picks up again in verse 34, for at the end of the seven years, as God had promised, Nebuchadnezzar was delivered from his affliction and restored to sanity and normal human life. It began with the king lifting his eyes to God, which suggests both faith and submission. "I lift up my eyes to you, to you whose throne is in heaven" (Ps. 123:1 NIV). "Look to Me, and be saved, all you ends of the earth!" (Isa. 45:22 NKJV). Some students believe that Nebuchadnezzar experienced spiritual conversion, and his testimony in these verses would seem to back that up. We have no idea what the king had learned about the God of Israel as he had listened to Daniel over those many years, but now the seed was producing fruit.

The first thing the king did was to praise the Lord (vv. 34–35). What a concise compendium of biblical theology this is, and what an exciting expression of worship! Theology and doxology belong together (Rom. 11:33–36), for spiritual experience that isn't based on truth is only superstition. The God of the Hebrews is the Most High God. Nebuchadnezzar's kingdom was limited, but God's kingdom includes everything in heaven and earth. Babylon would one day fall and give way to another empire, but God's kingdom will remain forever. Nothing can destroy His kingdom or defeat His purposes.

Seven years before, the king considered himself a great man and his kingdom a great kingdom, but now he had a different viewpoint. "All the peoples of the earth are regarded as nothing" (Dan. 4:35a NIV)—and that would include the king! Perhaps Daniel had quoted the prophet Isaiah to the king: "Behold, the nations are as a drop in a bucket, and are counted as the small dust on the scales.… It is He who sits above the circle of the earth, and its inhabitants are like grasshoppers" (Isa. 40:15, 22 NKJV).

The king acknowledged the sovereignty of God (v. 35b). This was the main lesson God wanted him to learn through this difficult experience (vv. 17, 25, 32). It's too bad that this wonderful Bible doctrine has been so maligned and misinterpreted by amateur Bible students, because an understanding of God's sovereignty brings the believer assurance, strength, comfort, and the kind of surrender that produces faith and freedom. The Bible teaches both divine sovereignty and human responsibility, and when you accept both, there is no contradiction or conflict. No person is more free than the believer who surrenders to the sovereign will of God. To ignore God's sovereignty is to exalt human responsibility and make man his own savior, but to deny responsibility is to make man a robot without accountability. The Bible preserves a beautiful balance that exalts God and enables His people to live joyously and victoriously no matter what the circumstances might be (Acts 4:23–31; Rom. 8:31–39).

Because God is sovereign, He can do as He pleases, and nobody can hinder Him or call Him to account (Rom. 9:14–23). The heart of sinful man rebels at the very idea of a sovereign God, for the human heart wants to be "free" of all outside control (Ps. 2:1–6). Sinners think they are "free" and don't realize how much they are in bondage to their fallen nature and to the forces of Satan and the world. Charles Spurgeon was very balanced in his theology, and he said:

> Most men quarrel with this [the sovereignty of God]. But mark, the thing that you complain of in God is the very thing that you love in yourselves.
>
> Every man likes to feel that he has a right to do with his own as he pleases. We all like to be little sovereigns. Oh, for a spirit that bows always before the sovereignty of God.[13]

The Most High God is so wise and powerful that He can ordain that His creatures have the freedom to make decisions and even disobey His revealed will, and yet He can accomplish His divine purposes on this earth. "Man's will is free because God is sovereign," said A. W. Tozer, who was not a confessed Calvinist. "A God less than sovereign could not bestow moral freedom upon His creatures. He would be afraid to do so."[14] Submitting to God's sovereign will didn't make Nebuchadnezzar any less of a man; in fact, this commitment transformed him from living like a beast to living like a man!

Finally, Nebuchadnezzar gave joyful witness to all peoples of the marvelous grace of God (vv. 1–3). In this preamble to the official account of his experience, the king extolled God's mighty wonders and His eternal kingdom, and he boldly announced that God had done great signs and wonders on his behalf. How different from Pharaoh's response to what the Lord did in Egypt! Instead of obeying the word given by Moses, Pharaoh saw God's power demonstrated in the plagues and continued to resist the Lord. He arrogantly declared, "Who is the LORD, that I should obey his voice to let Israel go? I know not the LORD, neither will I let Israel go" (Ex. 5:2). As a result of his rebellion, his country was ruined, thousands of people died, and Israel was still delivered from his power! When God isn't permitted to rule, He overrules and accomplishes His divine purposes for His glory.

What was the result of this "conversion" experience? God not only restored the king's reason and removed the beastly heart and mind, but He also graciously restored the king's honor and splendor and gave him back his throne! He testified that he "became even greater than before" (Dan. 4:36 NIV). Where sin had abounded, grace abounded even more (Rom. 5:20). Instead of boasting about his own accomplishments, Nebuchadnezzar said, "Now I Nebuchadnezzar praise and extol and honour the King of heaven" (Dan. 4:37).

He closed his official statement with a word of warning based on the lessons the Lord had taught him: "Those that walk in pride he [God] is able to abase" (v. 37). The world today doesn't think that pride is a wicked and dangerous sin, but instead practices flattery and exaggeration and exalts the words and the works of the "successful people" of the day. Some of them lack moral character, but as long as they are achievers, they get worldwide attention in the media. One day, the Lord will come in judgment, and His promise is this: "I will punish the world for its evil, the wicked for their sins. I will put an end to the arrogance of the haughty and will humble the pride of the ruthless" (Isa. 13:11 NIV).

Our Lord has the last word: "For whoever exalts himself will be humbled, and whoever humbles himself will be exalted" (Matt. 23:12 NIV).

QUESTIONS FOR PERSONAL REFLECTION
OR GROUP DISCUSSION

1. Describe a lesson that you or somebody you know learned the hard way.

2. List the risks you think Daniel may have faced in telling the king the bad news of the dream. *Rejection, King's anger, missunderstaning*

3. How does Daniel's courage in speaking God's truth to the king relate to our responsibility to speak God's Word in our world?
We need to be telling the truth.

4. What kind of burden do you think it would be to know the future and all the hard times that you were going to face over the next seven years?
I don't know

5. If you knew what hardships you were going to face, how do you think you would approach God differently? *Cautiously*

6. Nebuchadnezzar was warned of God's coming judgment and yet did nothing about it. What does that reveal to you about his faith?
had little

7. What keeps us (like the king) from repenting even when we are clear about our wrongdoing? *We want to keep our hands on the things of the world*

8. In what ways do you think our national leaders would lead differently if their hearts were more turned toward God?

   They would get on the side of truth

9. In what ways have you seen pride function as a destructive force?

   shooting, road rage

10. Think of a time when you were given a second chance at something. How do you suppose King Nebuchadnezzar approached his kingdom differently after receiving his second chance?

   He gave God more glory

Chapter Five

NUMBERED, WEIGHED, AND REJECTED

(Daniel 5)

Many people who know little or nothing about the Babylonians, Belshazzar's feast, or Daniel's prophecies use the phrase "the handwriting on the wall." The phrase comes from this chapter (v. 5) and announces impending judgment. Belshazzar, his wives and concubines, and a thousand notable guests were feasting and drinking while the army of the Medes and Persians waited at the city gates, ready to invade. The city of Babylon boasted that it was impregnable and that there was enough food stored away to feed the population for twenty years! But the Lord said that Babylon's time had come. "The LORD brings the counsel of the nations to nothing; He makes the plans of the peoples of no effect. The counsel of the LORD stands forever, the plans of His heart to all generations" (Ps. 33:10–11 NKJV). The will of God shall be done, no matter what.

We shall look at the persons involved in this drama and see how they related to the plan of God.

BELSHAZZAR—JUDGMENT DEFIED (5:1–4)

The great King Nebuchadnezzar died in 562 BC and was succeeded by his son Evil-Merodach, who reigned for only two years. His brother-in-law

Neriglissar murdered him in 560, usurped the throne, and ruled for four years. Then a weak puppet ruler (Labashi-Marduk) held the throne for two months, and finally Nabonidus became king and reigned from 556 to 539. Historians believe Nabonidus was married to a daughter of Nebuchadnezzar and was the father of Belshazzar. Nabonidus ruled the Babylonian Empire, but Belshazzar, his son, was coregent and ruled the city of Babylon.[1]

Indulgence (v. 1). Oriental despots took great pleasure in hosting great banquets and displaying their wealth and splendor (see Est. 1). Archaeologist tell us that there were halls in the city of Babylon adequate for gatherings this large and larger. This feast was a microcosm of the world system and focused on "the lust of the flesh, and the lust of the eyes, and the pride of life" (1 John 2:16). "What shall we eat?" and "What shall we drink?" are the questions most people want answered as they go through life (Matt. 6:25–34), and they're willing to follow anybody who will entertain them and gratify their appetites. Why worry about the enemy when you have security and plenty to eat?

Indifference (v. 1). Belshazzar knew that the army of the Medes and Persians was encamped outside the city, but he was indifferent to the danger that they posed. After all, the city was surrounded by a complex series of walls, some of them over three hundred feet high, and there were numerous defense towers on the walls. Could any army break through the fortified bronze gates? Wasn't there sufficient water for the people from the Euphrates River that flowed through the city from north to south, and wasn't there adequate food stored in the city? If ever a man was proud of his achievements and basked in self-confidence, it was Belshazzar. But it was a false confidence, not unlike what will happen to the people of this world before God declares war. "For when they say, 'Peace and safety!' then sudden destruction comes upon them" (1 Thess. 5:3 NKJV).

Belshazzar had been indifferent to the information God had given his grandfather Nebuchadnezzar in his famous dream (Dan. 2). It was decreed that the head of gold (Babylon) would be replaced by the breast and arms of silver (the Medo-Persian Empire). Daniel had seen this truth further verified in his vision recorded in Daniel 7, when he saw the Babylonian lion defeated by the Medo-Persian bear (vv. 1–5). This was in the first year of Belshazzar (v. 1). In his arrogant false confidence, Belshazzar was defying the will of God. "He says to himself, 'Nothing will shake me; I'll always be happy and never have trouble'" (Ps. 10:6 NIV).

Irreverence (vv. 2–4). Was the king drunk when he ordered the servants to bring in the consecrated vessels that had been taken from the temple in Jerusalem? (See 1:2; 2 Chron. 36:9–10.) His grandfather[2] Nebuchadnezzar had decreed that all peoples were to give respect to the God of the Jews (Dan. 3:29), and he himself had praised the Lord for His sovereignty and greatness (4:34–37). But as the years passed, the great king's words were forgotten, and his grandson Belshazzar treated the God of Israel with arrogant disrespect. Both the men and the women at the feast impudently used these valuable consecrated vessels like common drinking cups, and while they were drinking, they praised the false gods of Babylon! After all, the gods of Babylon had defeated the God of the Hebrews, so what was there to fear? Belshazzar and his guests could not have behaved more blasphemously. But people can defy the will of God and blaspheme His name only so long, and then the hand of the Lord begins to move.

THE LORD—JUDGMENT DECLARED (5:5–9)

"Do you not know this of old, since man was placed on earth, that the triumphing of the wicked is short, and the joy of the hypocrite is but for a moment? Though his haughtiness mounts up to the heavens, and his head reaches to the clouds, yet he will perish forever like his own refuse"

(Job 20:4–7 NKJV). Zophar's words didn't apply to Job, but they certainly applied to Belshazzar, and they apply today to anybody who defies the will of God.

Look at the wall (v. 5). Without warning, the fingers of a human hand appeared in an area of the plastered wall that was illuminated by a lampstand, and it must have been an awesome sight. The revelry gradually ceased, and the banquet hall became deathly quiet as the king and his guests stared in amazement at words being written on the wall. Both Hebrew and Aramaic are read from right to left, and the vowels must be supplied by the reader; but we aren't told whether the four words were written in a line

NSRHPLKTNMNM

or in a square to be read from the top down

PTMM
RKNN
SL ' '3

Whether the message followed either pattern or a different one, the writing was a miracle from the God of Israel that the idols of Babylon could never accomplish. "They have hands, but they handle not" (Ps. 115:7). It was the finger of God that defeated the Egyptians when Pharaoh refused to let the people go (Ex. 8:19), and the finger of God that wrote the holy law for Israel on the tablets of stone (31:18). Jesus said that He cast out demons "with the finger of God" (Luke 11:20), referring to the power of the Spirit (Matt. 12:28). Now the finger of God was writing a warning to the Babylonian leaders that the hand of God would very soon execute judgment.

Look at the king (vv. 6–7). Neither his exalted position nor his arrogant self-confidence could keep Belshazzar's face from turning pale, his heart from being overcome by terror, and his knees from knocking together. It must have been humiliating for the great ruler to be so out of control before so many important people. God had turned the banquet hall into a court-room and the king was about to be declared guilty. If the king couldn't control the moving fingers, at least he could try to understand the message, so he called for his wise men and commanded them to explain the mean-ing of the message on the wall, offering royal honors and gifts to the one who explained the message. He would wear a royal robe and a golden chain, both of which denoted authority, and he would become third ruler under Nabonidus and Belshazzar.

Look at the wise men (vv. 8–9). History repeats itself (2:10–13; 4:4–7) as the counselors confessed their inability to interpret the message on the wall. Even if they could have read the words, they didn't have the key to deciphering the meaning of the message. *Mene* could mean "mina," which was a measure of money, or the word *numbered*. *Tekel* could mean "shekel" (another unit of money) or the word *weighed*; and *peres* (the plu-ral is parsin) could mean "half-shekel," "half-mina," or the word *divided*. It could also refer to Persia!

The ignorance of the wise men made the king even more terrified, and his lords were perplexed and confused and could offer him no help. The time had come when political authority, wealth, power, and human wis-dom could do nothing to solve the problem. Once again, the Lord had exposed the ignorance of the world and the futility of human power to dis-cover and explain the mind and will of God.

THE QUEEN MOTHER—JUDGMENT DISREGARDED (5:10–12)

The rest of the palace heard about the crisis in the banquet hall, and when the news came to the queen mother, she immediately went to her son to offer counsel and encouragement. Her first words were, "Don't be alarmed! Don't look so pale!" (v. 10 NIV). Things aren't as bad as they appear to be!

She was optimistic about the whole situation and certain that, once the handwriting was accurately interpreted, everything would be fine. The American humorist Kin Hubbard once defined an optimist as "a person who believes that what's going to happen will be postponed."

Her attitude didn't match the gravity of the situation, but her suggestion was a good one: summon Daniel, the king's greatest adviser. Her words reveal another characteristic of King Belshazzar—ignorance. It seems incredible that he didn't know Daniel, one of the highest officers in Babylon, and certainly the wisest counselor in the empire. Belshazzar had been told about his grandfather's dreams and Daniel's interpretations (v. 22), but too often younger leaders are so concerned about themselves and the present that they forget to catch up on the past. Had young King Rehoboam listened to the counsel of the elders of Israel, he would have avoided a great deal of trouble (1 Kings 12).

The queen mother's description of Daniel certainly shows what God can do in and through dedicated people. Daniel brought "light and understanding and wisdom" into every situation and was able to explain mysteries, solve riddles, and unravel hard problems. His interpretations always proved correct and his prophecies were always fulfilled. During my many years of ministry, I have known a few men and women who were especially gifted in "understanding the times" and determining what the Lord wanted us to do. And yet every believer can claim the promise of James 1:5 and seek the mind of the Lord about any perplexing problem.

DANIEL—JUDGMENT DESCRIBED (5:13–29)

If he was sixteen when he was taken to Babylon in 605 BC, and Babylon fell to the Medes and Persians in 539, then Daniel was eighty-two years old when Belshazzar summoned him to the banquet hall, and perhaps he had been retired from royal service for many years. However, true servants of

God never abandon their ministries even in retirement but are always available to respond to God's call "in season, out of season" (2 Tim. 4:2).

The king's offer (vv. 13–17). To the king's shame, he knew Daniel only by name and reputation but did not know him personally. Yet Daniel had "done the king's business" in the third year of his reign (8:1, 27), which would have been 554 BC. What a tragedy that the ruler of the mighty city of Babylon should ignore one of the greatest men in history and turn to him only in the last hours of his life when it was too late. Had the queen mother told her son about this remarkable Jewish exile and yet he paid no attention? What kept the king so busy that he had no time to sit at the feet of God's prophet and learn from him the things that really mattered in life? "The older I grow, the more I distrust the familiar doctrine that age brings wisdom," wrote newspaper editor H. L. Mencken. But Daniel possessed much more than the human wisdom that comes from experience; he had the kind of supernatural knowledge and wisdom that can come only from God. How much Belshazzar could have learned from him!

The scenario wasn't a new one for Daniel: a revelation from God, a fearful and frustrated ruler, incompetent counselors, and God's servant to the rescue. He paid little attention to the king's flattering speech, and he had no use for the king's generous offer. Even if he had been younger, Daniel would have had no interest in either personal wealth or political power. "Not greedy for money" is one of the qualifications of a servant of God (1 Tim. 3:3 NKJV; see 1 Peter 5:2). Along with Daniel, servants like Moses (Num. 16:15), Samuel (1 Sam. 12:3), and Paul (Acts 20:33) exemplify this unselfish attitude. They simply were not for sale.

The prophet's rebuke (vv. 18–24). Daniel was respectful to the king but he was not afraid to tell him the truth. Even if we don't respect the officer and the way he or she lives, we must respect the office, for "the powers that be are ordained of God" (Rom. 13:1). From the very beginning of their lives in Babylon (Dan. 1), Daniel and his friends had always exercised humility and tact when dealing with the authorities, and because of this, God blessed them. "Sound speech, that cannot be condemned" (Titus 2:8) is standard equipment for the obedient servant of God.

The king didn't know Daniel personally, but Daniel certainly knew the personal life of the king! He knew of his pride and his knowledge of the history of his grandfather, but Daniel reviewed that history just the same. "Those who do not remember the past are condemned to relive it," wrote philosopher George Santayana, and Belshazzar qualified. The lesson that Nebuchadnezzar learned and that his grandson Belshazzar heard about but ignored was that "the most high God ruled in the kingdom of men" (Dan. 5:21). The God of Israel alone is the true and living God and rules sovereignly in all the affairs of this world, including the affairs of the great empire of Babylon!

Nebuchadnezzar showed his pride by boasting about his achievements and taking credit for what God had helped him accomplish (4:29–30), but his grandson displayed his pride by desecrating the holy vessels from the temple of the Most High God and treating the Lord with contempt. By using the vessels of the true God to praise the idols of Babylon, the king was guilty of both blasphemy and idolatry; by ignoring what he knew of Babylonian royal history, he displayed his ignorance. Belshazzar acted as though he was in command and his life would go on for many more years, yet the very breath in his mouth was controlled by the hand of God (5:23). "For in him we live, and move, and have our being" (Acts 17:28). "This night your soul will be required of you" (Luke 12:20 NKJV).

Like King Belshazzar and his guests, many people in our world today are unmindful of the lessons of the past, unintelligent when it comes to interpreting the present, and totally unprepared for the consequences that lie in the future.

The Lord's warning (vv. 25–29). Anyone who knew Aramaic could have read the words written on the wall, but Daniel was able to interpret their meaning and apply God's revelation to the people in the banquet hall, especially the king. Daniel didn't interpret the words to signify units of money (mina, shekel, half-mina, or half-shekel) but to convey warning to the king. The word *mina* meant "numbered," and the repetition of the word indicated that God had determined and established the end of the kingdom and it would happen shortly (Gen. 41:32). Babylon's days were numbered! More than that, *tekel* indicated that the king himself had been weighed by God and found wanting; so the king's days were numbered. Who would bring an end to the kingdom and the king of Babylon? The answer was in the third word, *peres,* which carried a double meaning: "divided" and "Persia." Babylon would be divided between the Medes and the Persians, whose armies were at the gates of the city that very night.

There are times when God gives warnings in order to bring sinners to repentance, such as when he sent Jonah to Nineveh (Jonah 3); but there are also times when His warnings are final and divine judgment is determined. When God warned Nebuchadnezzar about his pride and unconcern for the poor, He gave the king a year in which to repent and seek God's forgiveness (Dan. 4:28–33). The king refused to humble himself and judgment fell. But when Daniel confronted Belshazzar, he offered him no way of escape.

Even though Daniel didn't want the rewards, the king kept his promise and clothed him in royal purple, hung the golden chain around his neck, and declared that he was third ruler in the kingdom. Daniel didn't protest; he knew that the city would fall that very night and that the conquerors wouldn't care who was in office. They were now in command.

Darius—Judgment Delivered (5:30–31)

The phrase "that very night" (v. 30 NIV) has an ominous ring to it. "He who is often rebuked, and hardens his neck, will suddenly be destroyed, and that without remedy" (Prov. 29:1 NKJV). Belshazzar was slain that very night and the head of gold was replaced by the arms and chest of silver. According to historians, the date was October 12, 539 BC.

The conquest of Babylon was engineered by Cyrus, king of Persia (1:21; 6:28; 10:1; and see 2 Chron. 36:22–23; Ezra 3—5, *passim*), who was God's chosen servant for the task (Isa. 44:28; 45:1–4). Who then was "Darius the Mede," mentioned in Daniel (Dan. 5:31; 6:1, 9, 25, 28; 9:1)? Many students believe that Darius was Gubaru, an important officer in the army whom Cyrus made ruler of the province of Babylon. Darius the Mede must not be confused with Darius I, who ruled from 522 to 486 and encouraged the Jewish remnant in the restoration of the temple (Ezra 5—6).[4]

Because of the high walls, the guard towers, and the strong bronze gates, the people in the city of Babylon thought they were safe from the enemy; but the Medo-Persian army found a way to get into the city. The Euphrates River flowed through Babylon from north to south, and by diverting the stream, the army was able to go under the city gates and into the city. The conquest of Babylon and its ultimate destruction had been predicted by Isaiah (Isa. 13—14; 21; 47) and Jeremiah (Jer. 50—51). Babylon had been God's chosen instrument to chasten His people Israel, but the Babylonian army had carried things too far and mistreated the Jews (50:33–34). The conquest of Babylon was also God's punishment for what they had done to His temple (50:28; 51:11).

The prophecies were fulfilled and ancient Babylon is no more, but "mystery Babylon" is still with us (Rev. 17:5, 7; 18:2, 10). Throughout Scripture, Babylon (the rebel city) is contrasted to Jerusalem (the Holy City). Babylon was founded by Nimrod, a rebel against the Lord (Gen. 10:8–10). It is seen in Scripture as the great city of this world, while Jerusalem symbolizes the eternal city of God. Revelation 17 and 18 describe the rise and fall of "mystery Babylon" in the end times, the satanic system that will seduce the world's peoples and entice them to reject the message of God and live for the sinful pleasures of this life. If you compare Jeremiah 50—51 with Revelation 18, you will see many similarities between the Babylon of ancient history and the Babylon of future prophecy. The future Babylonian world system will help Antichrist, the man of sin, rise to power in this world, but his kingdom will be destroyed by Jesus Christ when He returns to reign (19:11–21).

Years ago, Dr. Harry Rimmer published a book on prophecy called *Straight Ahead Lies Yesterday*, a title that could well be given to the book of Daniel. The world has always had its great cities, its mighty empires, and its powerful dictators, but the Most High God still reigns in heaven and on the earth and accomplishes His purposes. No nation, leader, or individual citizen can long resist Almighty God and win the battle.

On the occasion of Queen Victoria's Diamond Jubilee in 1897, poet and novelist Rudyard Kipling wrote a poem titled "Recessional." It wasn't received with great applause and approval because he warned the celebrating nation (and empire) that God was in charge and that pride eventually leads to defeat. One stanza reads:

> The tumult and the shouting dies;
> The captains and the kings depart—
> Still stands Thine ancient Sacrifice,
> An humble and a contrite heart.
> Lord God of Hosts, be with us yet,
> Lest we forget—lest we forget!

Belshazzar forgot the Word of God and the lessons of history and lost his kingdom and his life.

May we not make the same mistakes today!

QUESTIONS FOR PERSONAL REFLECTION
OR GROUP DISCUSSION

1. In what kinds of situations do you usually hear people say, "I saw the handwriting on the wall"?

2. Describe your perspective on why having plenty to eat and drink (our physical needs met) often causes us to turn away from God.

When our needs are met we think we do not need God

3. What examples do you see today of the kind of irreverence the king showed in using something sacred in an unholy way?

The way people treat marriages, government days of rest

4. God stopped the party in its tracks with the miracle of the handwriting on the wall. What kinds of things have you experienced from God that stopped you (or someone you know) in your tracks?

5. When you feel God step into your life as the king did, how do you usually respond?

My response is, here am I send me

6. What do you think it takes for a Christian to achieve the kind of reputation Daniel had?

Honestly, bravely, friendly

7. How could understanding the past (his grandfather's encounters with God) have helped Belshazzar understand the present more clearly?

If he understood how God was with Nebucavezzar, he would have respects

8. In what ways do you see spiritual values pass down (or not) through generations?

9. What lessons from history do you think stand as particularly relevant reminders to us today?

10. When God brings us up short, as He did the people in this account, what is our best response?

Chapter Six

LIARS, LAWS, AND LIONS

(Daniel 6)

Darius the Mede must not be confused with Darius I, who ruled Persia from 522 to 486 and during whose reign the temple was restored by the Jewish remnant at Jerusalem. Darius the Mede was probably the name (or title) of the man King Cyrus appointed ruler of the city of Babylon (9:1) until he himself took charge; or it may have been the title Cyrus himself took when he came to reign.[1] King Cyrus ruled the Persian empire from 539 to 530 and was succeeded by Cambyses (530–522).

As is often the case after a conquest, the new ruler wants to reorganize the government of the conquered kingdom so as to establish his authority and make things conform to his own leadership goals. But when Darius began to reorganize Babylon, he brought to light a conflict between his officers and Daniel, a veteran administrator who was now in his eighties. Today, wherever you find dedicated believers living and working with unbelievers, you will often see the same forces at work that are described in this chapter, whether in families, churches, corporations, or governments.

HONESTY VERSUS CORRUPTION (6:1–4)

Darius must have suspected that the officers he had inherited were not doing their work faithfully but were robbing him of wealth, and his suspicions were correct. It was impossible for Darius to keep his hands on everything in the empire, because that would have involved supervising every worker, auditing every account, and checking on every assignment. The king had to depend on his officers to see that the work was done well, and this meant he had to appoint officers he could trust. Darius was a man experienced in the ways of the world, and he knew that there was plenty of opportunity for graft in the Babylonian government (see Eccl. 5:8–9).

A wise leader first gathers information, and Darius soon learned about Daniel and the reputation he had for honesty and wisdom, what the KJV calls "an excellent spirit" (Dan. 6:3). It's likely that Daniel was in semiretirement at this time, but the king appointed him to be one of three key administrators over the kingdom. These three men were to manage the affairs of the 120 leaders who ruled over the provinces[2] and to report directly to the king. Daniel proved to be such a superior worker that Darius planned to make him his number-one administrator over the entire kingdom.

When the other leaders heard about this plan, it irritated them and they tried to find something wrong in his work, but nothing could be found. They opposed Daniel for several reasons, including just plain envy; but their main concern was financial. They knew that with Daniel in charge, they wouldn't be able to use their offices for personal profit and would lose their share of the graft that could go into their pockets. It's also likely that these younger men resented an older man—and a Jewish exile at that—telling them what to do and checking on their work. It was another case of anti-Semitism, a grievous sin that is found in Scripture from the days of Pharaoh to the end times (Rev. 12). Apparently these officers didn't know God's covenant with Abraham that promised to bless those who blessed the Jews and curse those who cursed them (Gen. 12:1–3). When these men started to attack Daniel, they were asking for God's judgment.

It isn't always the case that the honest employee gets the promotion while his enemies are judged. Joseph and Daniel were both promoted by pagan rulers, but I have a friend who was fired because he worked too hard! Apparently his Christian integrity and his diligent work showed up the laziness of the other workers, so the foreman found reason to dismiss him. However, it's better to maintain your integrity and testimony than to sacrifice them just to keep your job. If we put the Lord first, He'll care for us, even if we don't get the promotion (Matt. 6:33). Many a faithful Christian has been bypassed for promotion or a salary increase just because somebody higher up didn't like him, but the workers' rewards will one day come from the hand of the Lord.

BELIEVING VERSUS SCHEMING (6:5–11)

It's certainly a commendable thing when people possess character so impeccable that they can't be accused of doing wrong except in matters relating to their faith. The conniving officers could never tempt Daniel to do anything illegal, but they could attempt to make his faithful religious practices illegal. Daniel didn't hide the fact that he prayed in his home three times each day with his windows opened toward Jerusalem (v. 10), and his enemies knew this. If the king made prayer to other gods illegal, then Daniel was as good as in the lions' den!

The king's response (vv. 5–9). King Darius must have been impressed when 122 government officials assembled in his throne room to have an audience with him. Of course, Daniel wasn't there, even though he was chief among the administrators; but the leaders had been careful not to include him. However, they deceptively included him in their speech, for they claimed that all the royal administrators had agreed on the plan presented to Darius. In fact, they included all the officers in the empire— "administrators, prefects, satraps, advisers and governors" (v. 7 NIV)—to give the king the impression that his leaders were united behind him and desirous of magnifying him and his office. The men who hatched the plot probably had not consulted with the lesser officers throughout the empire, but these officers weren't likely to disagree with the plan. Anything that pleased the king would only strengthen their positions.

The administrators were very clever in the plot they conceived and the way they presented it. They knew that Darius wanted to unify the kingdom and as quickly as possible transform the defeated Babylonians into loyal Persians. What better way than to focus on the great king himself and make him not just the supreme leader but the only god for an entire month! To emphasize the importance of this law, the officers requested the ultimate sentence: Anyone who didn't obey it would be thrown into a den of lions. Of course, their flattery fed the king's pride, and he quickly agreed with them, had the law written out, and signed it. Once it was signed, the law could not be changed or nullified (vv. 8, 12, 15; Est. 1:19).

There's every evidence that Darius loved and appreciated Daniel, but in his haste, the king had put his friend in peril. It has well been said that flattery is manipulation, not communication, and in his pride, Darius succumbed to the flattery of evil men. "For there is no faithfulness in their mouth; their inward part is very wickedness; their throat is an open sepulchre; they flatter with their tongue" (Ps. 5:9).

Daniel's response (vv. 10–11). The scheming officers lost no time in proclaiming the king's decree. Daniel probably prayed "evening and morning and at noon" (Ps. 55:17 NKJV),[3] and his enemies wanted to use the earliest opportunity to arrest him. The sooner Daniel was out of the way, the sooner they could start running the country for their own profit. When Daniel prayed toward the Holy City and the temple, he was claiming the prayer promise that Solomon stated when he dedicated the temple (1 King 8:28–30, 38–39, 46–51). Jonah claimed this same promise when he was in the belly of the great fish (Jonah 2:4). The exiled Jews no longer had a temple or priesthood, but God was still on the throne and would hear their cries for help.

During the first year of Darius, Daniel had learned from the book of Jeremiah that the Jewish captivity would end after seventy years, and he turned this great promise into prayer (Dan. 9:1ff.). Daniel was interceding for his people and asking God to keep His promise and deliver them. Like the plot against the Jews recorded in the book of Esther, the plot against Daniel the intercessor was an attack on the whole Jewish nation.

Had he not been a man of faith and courage, Daniel could have compromised and found excuses for not maintaining his faithful prayer life. He might have closed his windows and prayed silently three times a day until the month was over, or he could have left the city and prayed somewhere else. But that would have been unbelief and cowardice; he would have been scheming just like the enemy, and the Lord would have withheld His blessing. No, a man like Daniel feared only the Lord; and when you fear the Lord, you need not fear anyone else. "We ought to obey God rather than men" (Acts 5:29 NKJV). Some of the leaders spied on him, heard him pray, and brought the report to the king.

The most important part of a believer's life is the part that only God sees, our daily private time of meditation and prayer. "You pray as your face is set," said British theologian P. T. Forsythe, "towards Jerusalem or Babylon." Most of the world begins the day looking toward the world and hoping to get something from it, but the Christian believer looks to the Lord and His promises and enters each new day by faith. Outlook determines outcome, and when we look to the Lord for His guidance and help each day, we know that the outcome is in His hands and that we have nothing to fear. "Real true faith is man's weakness leaning on God's strength," said D. L. Moody, and we might add, man's weakness transformed into God's strength (Heb. 11:34).

GOD'S POWER VERSUS MAN'S AUTHORITY (6:12–23)

Three times a day for many years, Daniel had prayed, given thanks, and made supplication (vv. 10–11), which is the same pattern Paul instructed us to follow (Phil. 4:6–7). No wonder Daniel had such peace and courage! Ernest Wadsworth, a champion of effective prayer, said, "Pray for a faith that will not shrink when washed in the waters of affliction." Daniel had that kind of faith. He had walked with the Lord for more than eighty years and knew that his God wouldn't fail him. Hadn't the Lord helped him stand true during his time of training? Didn't the Lord save his life by giving him the wisdom he needed to interpret the king's dream, and didn't the Lord deliver his three friends out of the fiery furnace? Daniel had a copy of the prophecy of Jeremiah (Dan. 9:2), so he must have read: "Behold, I am the LORD, the God of all flesh: is there any thing too hard for me?" (Jer. 32:27). No doubt he responded with "there is nothing too hard for thee" (v. 17). A believer who knows how to kneel in prayer has no problem standing in the strength of the Lord.

Daniel accused (vv. 12–13). The men who had spied on Daniel hurried to inform Darius that his favorite officer had disobeyed the law and shown disrespect to the king. It's remarkable how people can work together quickly to do evil but find it difficult to get together to do anything good. "Their feet are swift to shed blood" (Rom. 3:15). They showed no respect to Daniel, who held a higher office than they did, but disdainfully called him "one of the exiles from Judah" (Dan. 6:13 NIV). These proud men didn't realize that God was with His exiled people and within the next twenty-four hours would vindicate His servant.

As they take their stand for what is right and what the Lord has commanded them to do, God's people in every age have been falsely accused, cruelly persecuted, and unjustly killed. "Yes, and all who desire to live godly in Christ Jesus will suffer persecution" (2 Tim. 3:12 NKJV). The Puritan preacher Henry Smith said, "God examines with trials, the devil with temptations and the world with persecutions." Another Puritan, Richard Baxter, said that God's people should be more concerned that they deserved the persecution than that they be delivered from it, because deserving it would be evidence of their faithfulness to the Lord.

The king distressed (vv. 14–18). The king was distressed mainly because Daniel was both his friend and his greatest help in the governing of the empire, and he didn't want to sign his death warrant. But Darius was also distressed because of the way he had acted. His pride had gotten the best of him, he had believed the lies of the leaders, and had hastily signed the law. Had Darius taken time to consult with Daniel, he would have discovered the plot; but perhaps the Lord allowed events to proceed as they did so that Daniel's enemies could be exposed and judged. God works "all things after the counsel of his own will" (Eph. 1:11) and He knows what He is doing.

The king made it clear that he wanted to save Daniel from execution, but all his efforts failed. The situation is similar to the one described in the book of Esther: Once the law had been signed, nothing could change it. Since Darius was a "god" and the people were praying to him, how could he make any mistakes? And how could a "god" not punish someone who had broken one of his laws? Furthermore, the laws of the Medes and Persians couldn't be annulled or changed. For the entire day, Darius ignored all other matters concerning the kingdom and tried to free Daniel, but his attempts all failed. Of course, Daniel's enemies were on hand to remind the king that he had to enforce the law whether he liked it or not. At the end of the day, Darius had to call Daniel and have him put in the lions' den.

The lions' den was a large pit divided by a moveable wall that could be pulled up to allow the lions to go from one side to the other. The keeper would put food in the empty side and lift up the wall so the lions would cross over and eat. He would quickly lower the wall and clean the safe side of the pit. The animals weren't fed often or great amounts of food so that their appetites would be keen in case there was to be an execution. Living at the gnawing edge of hunger didn't make them too tame!

Before Daniel was lowered into the pit and the wall lifted up, the king offered a prayer that Daniel's God would deliver him because Daniel was faithful to serve Him continually (Dan. 6:16; see v. 20; 3:17). He then had the pit covered and the rock sealed so that everything was done according to the law. Nobody would dare break the king's official seal, so that when the pit was opened, everybody would have to confess that God had performed a great miracle. It makes us think of the stone at our Lord's tomb that was sealed by the Roman authorities, and yet Jesus came forth alive!

The king had a bad night, not unlike the night Xerxes experienced in the story of Esther (Est. 6:1ff.). Oriental kings were given all kinds of diversions to entertain them and help them relax and go to sleep, but Darius refused all of them. He spent a sleepless night and even fasted! He wondered if the Lord would deliver the old Jewish prophet from the lions' den.

The Lord victorious (vv. 19–23). Darius arose with the first light of dawn and hastened to the lions' den. Even before he got to the pit and ordered the seals broken and the stone removed, he called out to Daniel in an anguished voice. In what he said, he confessed that Daniel's God was the living God, not a dead idol, and that He had the power to deliver His faithful servant. Daniel's faith brought him peace and assurance, but the king's faith was weak and wavering. "Is your God able to deliver you?"[4] When Darius heard Daniel's voice saying "O king, live forever," he knew that his friend and faithful officer and been delivered (Heb. 11:33).

Daniel was always quick to give God the glory (Dan. 6:22; see 2:27–28; 4:25; 5:21–23). God could have closed the lions' mouths by simply saying the word, but He chose to send an angel to do the job. The angel not only controlled the hungry beasts but also kept Daniel company, just as the Lord had come to walk with the three Jewish men whom Nebuchadnezzar had thrown into the fiery furnace (3:24–25). The book of Daniel reveals a great deal about the work of angels in this world, not only their ministries to God's people but also their influence on nations (10:10–13, 20–21). When we think of an angel delivering Daniel, promises like Psalms 34:7 and 91:11 come to mind, and we remember the angels' ministry to Jesus (Mark 1:13; Luke 22:43). We don't know when angels are with us (Heb. 13:2), but we do know that they are present to serve us and sent by God to assist us (1:14). When Daniel was removed from the lions' den, he bore no wounds, just as the three Jewish men bore no evidence they had even been in the furnace (Dan. 3:27).

The Lord delivered Daniel because of his faith (6:23) and because he was innocent of any crime before the king or any sin before the Lord (v. 22). This means that the king's law about prayer was rejected in heaven and that Daniel was right in disobeying it. By suggesting such a law, the scheming officers disobeyed the true and living God (Ex. 20:1–6) and robbed Him of the glory He deserved. God saved Daniel because it brought great glory to His name and also because he still had more work to do. God's servants are immortal until their work is done.

However, it must be pointed out that not every faithful servant of the Lord is delivered from trial and death in some miraculous way. Hebrews 11:1–35 names some great men and women of faith and describes their achievements, but verses 36–40 describe the "others" who also had great faith and yet were persecuted and martyred. These unnamed "others" had just as much faith as the people in the first group but were not granted special deliverance. James the brother of John was martyred, but Peter was delivered from prison (Acts 12), yet both men were apostles and faithful servants of the Lord. It's unwise to draw conclusions from consequences lest we end up making wrong evaluations (Acts 14:8–20; 28:1–6).⁵

GOD'S GLORY VERSUS MAN'S DISGRACE (6:24–28)

Daniel's night of confinement in the lions' den ended in a morning of glory and deliverance, with the king himself setting him free. Imagine the excitement in the city as the news spread that Daniel had spent the night in the lions' den and had come out unhurt. God could have prevented Daniel from going into the lions' den, but by allowing him to go in and bringing him out unhurt, the Lord received greater honor.

The traitors were judged (v. 24). Eastern monarchs had absolute power over their subjects (5:19), and no one dared to question their decisions, let alone try to change them. Darius didn't throw all 122 officers and their families into the den of lions but only those men and their families who had accused Daniel (6:11–13). "The righteous is delivered from trouble, but the wicked takes his place" (Prov. 11:8 NASB). The only exception to this law occurred when Jesus Christ the Righteous One took the place of guilty sinners when He died for them on the cross (1 Peter 3:18).

There is a law of compensation that says, "Whoever digs a pit will fall into it, and he who rolls a stone will have it roll back on him" (Prov. 26:27 NKJV). For example, Pharaoh ordered the Hebrew male babies destroyed in Egypt, and at Passover, all the Egyptian firstborn died. He commanded the newborn Jewish babies to be drowned in the Nile River, and his own army was drowned in the Red Sea (Ex. 14—15). Haman tried to destroy the Jewish nation and ended up being hanged on the gallows he had made for Mordecai (Est. 7:9–10; 9:25). Even if sinners aren't judged in this present life, they will be judged after they die (Heb. 9:27), and the judgment will be just.

It seems cruel to us that the families were destroyed along with the conspirators, but that was an official Persian law and the conspirators knew it. Jewish law prohibited punishing the children for the sins of the fathers (Deut. 24:16; Ezek. 18:20), but Eastern despots took a different view. They didn't want any remaining member of a traitor's family to conspire to kill the ruler who ordered the father's execution. It was much easier to bury corpses than to keep an eye on potential assassins, and besides, the example put fear into the hearts of potential troublemakers. Another important factor is God's covenant with Abraham. The Lord promised that those who blessed the people of Israel would themselves be blessed, but those who cursed them would be cursed (Gen. 12:1–3).[6] In allowing the families to be slain, God was only being faithful to His Word.

The Lord was glorified (vv. 25–27). But Darius did more than execute the criminals. He also issued a decree to the whole empire, commanding his subjects to show fear and reverence to the God of Daniel, the God of the Hebrew exiles (vv. 25–27). Darius's first decree in this chapter declared that he was god (vv. 7–9), but this second decree declared that the God of the Hebrews was the true and living God! In doing this, Darius joined King Nebuchadnezzar by giving public testimony to the power and glory of the true and living God (2:47; 3:28–29; 4:1–3, 34–37). God could have kept Daniel out of the lions' den, but by rescuing him from the lions, God received greater glory.

The Jews had been humiliated by the destruction of Jerusalem and the temple because their defeat made it look as though the false gods of the Babylonians were stronger than the true God of Israel. The idolatry of the Jewish people, especially their kings and priests, had brought about the ruin of Judah, and the Lord used an idolatrous nation to defeat them. Jehovah hadn't been honored by His own people, but now He was receiving praise from pagan rulers whose decrees would be published throughout the Gentile world. These decrees were a witness to the Gentiles that there was but one true God, the God of the Jews; but the decrees were also a reminder to the Jews that Jehovah was the true and living God. The Jewish exiles were surrounded by idols and were constantly tempted to worship the gods of the conquerors. What a paradox that the Jews, who were supposed to be witnesses to the Gentiles of the true and living God, were being witnessed to by the Gentiles!

The theology expressed in the decree of Darius is as true as anything written by Moses, David, or Paul. Jehovah is the living and eternal God whose kingdom will never be destroyed (v. 26; see Deut. 5:26; Josh. 3:10; Ps. 42:2; Jer. 10:10; Ps. 145:13; Rev. 11:15). He is the God who saves people and rescues them from danger and death, and who performs signs and wonders (Dan. 6:27; see 3:28–29; 4:3; Deut. 6:22; Neh. 9:10; Ps. 105:26–36; 135:9; Jer. 32:20–21).

God's servant prospered (v. 28). Since Darius the Mede is a "shadowy figure" in ancient history, we aren't sure how long he ruled Babylon and exactly when Cyrus took over the throne personally. It's been suggested that since Darius was sixty-two years old when he took Babylon (5:31), he may have died within a few years, and then Cyrus ascended the throne. Regardless of what transpired, Daniel was respected by Darius and Cyrus and continued to be a witness for the Lord. He lived to see Cyrus issue the edict that permitted the Jews to return to their land and rebuild their temple (2 Chron. 36:22–23; Ezra 1:1–4) and may have been used of God to help bring about this fulfillment of Jeremiah's prophecy (Dan. 9:1–2; Jer. 25:11–12). Certainly his prayers for his people played an important role in the positive attitude Cyrus had toward the Jewish people.

Along with the account of the deliverance of the three men from the fiery furnace (Dan. 3), the report of Daniel's deliverance from the lions' den must have brought great encouragement to the Jews in exile. They knew about Jeremiah's prophecy and wondered if their God would really deliver them. But if He could deliver three men from a furnace and Daniel from the lions, surely He could deliver the exiles from Babylon and take them back to their own land.

But Daniel has a message for God's people today who are being attacked by the enemy and suffering because of their righteous stand for the Lord. Whether we face the fiery furnace (1 Peter 1:6–8; 4:12–19) or the roaring lion (5:8–10), we are in the Lord's care and He will work out His divine purposes for His glory. "Casting all your care upon Him, for He cares for you" (v. 7 NKJV).

QUESTIONS FOR PERSONAL REFLECTION
OR GROUP DISCUSSION

1. Chapter 6 describes a time of reorganization. What are the stresses and fears that take place during a reorganization of any type?

   The fears of the unknown, the adjusting of change

2. Describe a time when you (or someone you know) have experienced difficulties at work that related directly to your religious beliefs.

   My dad left the AC factory

3. How do you think you would have handled it if you had been Daniel and prayer had been outlawed?

   I would have hope I would do what Daniel did

4. In what ways do you agree or disagree with the statement, "The most important part of a believer's life is the part that only God sees"?

   God is interested in our heart

5. Daniel had some experiences to look back on and remain convinced of God's faithfulness. What experiences do you look back on to remember God's faithfulness?

6. Daniel faced lions because of his beliefs. What are the penalties that Christians today face because of their beliefs?

7. An angel protected Daniel. In what ways have you seen evidence of the work of angels in your life? *our troubles*

8. In this account, the bad guys "get it" in the end. How often do you see that happen in your experience?

9. If God receives glory from miraculous rescues and good-guy endings, why do you think the righteous still suffer?

10. What would you say is the key to giving God glory no matter how our circumstances turn out? *Praise God for visitations his rebukes*

Chapter Seven

"THY KINGDOM COME"

(Daniel 7)

K ing Nabonidus was monarch over the empire, but he made his son Belshazzar ruler over Babylon; and the first year of his reign was probably 553. This means that the events described in chapters 7 and 8 preceded those described in chapters 5 and 6, and Daniel was nearly seventy years old at the time these events occurred. Perhaps Daniel arranged the material in his book this way so that the records of his interpretations of the dreams and visions of others came before the visions that the Lord gave to him (7:1–2; 8:1; 9:20–27; 10:1ff.). Except for Nebuchadnezzar's dream of the great image explained in chapter 2, the other visions in Daniel 2—6 don't have the wide sweep of application as do the visions granted to Daniel. The vision explained in Daniel 7 parallels the vision God gave to Nebuchadnezzar in chapter 2.

In this vision, Daniel learned about six different kingdoms, four of them kingdoms of this world, one of them the kingdom of Satan, and the last one the kingdom of Messiah.

THE KINGDOMS OF THIS WORLD (7:1–7, 15–23)

God communicated with Daniel while he was asleep by giving him disturbing visions in a dream (vv. 1–2, 15). During this vision, Daniel was also a part of the event because he was able to approach an angel and ask for an interpretation (v. 16). Daniel doesn't explain how he could be asleep in his bed and yet be able to speak to an angel standing before the throne of God. Perhaps like Paul, he didn't know if he was in the body or out of the body (see 8:2; 2 Cor. 12:1–3).

The restless sea is a frequent biblical image for the nations of the world (Isa. 17:12–13; 57:20; 60:5; Ezek. 26:3; Rev. 13:1; 17:15). Just as the ocean is sometimes stormy, so the nations of the world are sometimes in confusion or even at war; and just as the waves and currents of the ocean are unpredictable, so the course of world history is beyond man's ability to chart or predict. Historians like Oswald Spengler and Arnold Toynbee have attempted to find a pattern to world history, but to no avail. From the human point of view, the nations seem to work out their own destinies, but the invisible winds of God blow over the surface of the water to accomplish His will in His time. If there's one message that is empha-sized in the book of Daniel it's that "the Most High rules in the kingdom of men" (4:32 NKJV).

The angel told Daniel that the four beasts represented four kingdoms (7:17), the same sequence of empires that Nebuchadnezzar had seen in his dream (chap. 2). However, the king saw a great and impressive image made of valuable metals, while Daniel saw dangerous beasts that ruthlessly devoured peoples and nations. To human eyes, the nations of the world are like Nebuchadnezzar's great image, impressive and important; but from God's viewpoint, the nations are only ferocious beasts that attack and seek to devour one another.

The lion with the wings of an eagle (v. 4). This represented the empire of Babylon, which in Nebuchadnezzar's image was the head of gold (2:37–38). In Scripture, Babylon is identified with both the lion and the eagle

(Jer. 4:7, 13; 48:40; 49:19–22; 50:17; Ezek. 17:3, 12; see also Hab. 1:6–8). The description of the lion being lifted up to stand like a man, and then given a man's heart, reminds us of how God humbled King Nebuchadnezzar and made him live like a beast for seven years (Dan. 4:16, 28–34). God told Daniel that the Babylonian Empire would fall.

The bear with three ribs in its mouth (v. 5). This symbolized the empire of the Medes and Persians who defeated Babylon (Dan. 5) and parallels the arms and chest of silver in the great image (2:39). The bear was raised up on one side because the Persians were stronger than the Medes. In the later vision of the ram with two horns (Dan. 8), the higher horn represented the Persians (vv. 3, 20). Interpreters aren't agreed on the meaning of the three ribs that the bear carried in its mouth. The best explanation is that they stand for Lydia, Egypt, and Babylon, nations that the Medes and Persians had conquered. The armies of the Medo-Persian Empire did indeed "devour much flesh" as they marched across the battlefields.

The leopard with four wings (v. 6). This represented Alexander the Great and the swift conquests of his army, resulting in the incredible expansion of the kingdom of Greece. This beast is identified with the number four: four heads and four horns (see 8:8, 21–22). Alexander's untimely death in 323 left him without a successor, and his kingdom was divided into four parts and assigned to his leaders. Palestine and Egypt went to Ptolemy I; Syria was ruled by Seleucus I; Thrace and Asia Minor were assigned to Lysimachus; and Macedon and Greece were governed by Antipater and Cassander.

The "dreadful and terrible" beast (v. 7). This represented the Roman Empire, as strong and enduring as iron and as uncompromising as a beast on the rampage. The Roman armies swept across the ancient world and defeated one nation after another until the empire extended from the Atlantic Ocean east to the Caspian Sea and from North Africa north to the Rhine and Danube Rivers. Egypt, Palestine, and Syria were all under Roman domination.

This beast corresponds with the legs of iron on Nebuchadnezzar's image (2:40–43), but the ten toes (ten kings, vv. 43–44) are represented by ten horns (7:7, 24). Often in Scripture, a horn is a symbol of a ruler or of royal authority (1 Sam. 2:10; Ps. 132:17). Later in this study we will have more to say about the "little horn" of Daniel 7:8.

In the great movement of ancient history, one empire has replaced another, leading up to the establishing of the Roman Empire. The two visions (chaps. 2 and 7) make it clear that God knows the future and controls the rise and fall of nations and rulers. Daniel was then living in the Babylonian Empire, but he knew that Babylon would be taken by the Medes and Persians, and that Greece would conquer the Medo-Persian Empire, and Rome would eventually conquer all. Prophecy is history written beforehand.

THE KINGDOM OF SATAN (7:8, 11–12, 21–26)

The four kingdoms represented by the four beasts have already come and gone; however, verse 12 indicates that each kingdom continues to exist in some way within the succeeding kingdom that "devoured" it. But Daniel saw in his vision something that wasn't revealed to Nebuchadnezzar: The last human kingdom on earth would be a frightful kingdom, unlike any of the previous kingdoms, and it would even declare war on God! This is the kingdom of Antichrist, described in Revelation 13—19, an evil kingdom that will be destroyed when Jesus Christ returns to earth. This judgment was depicted in Nebuchadnezzar's vision as the stone cut "out without hands" that tumbled down the mountain and destroyed the image (Dan. 2:34–35, 44–45).

The ten horns (vv. 7–8, 24; Rev. 13:1; 17:3, 7, 12, 16). These represent ten kings or kingdoms that will exist in the last days. Daniel wrote in language the people of his day could understand, and the concept of nations as we have them today would be foreign to the ancients. In Daniel's day countries were ruled by kings, but the "kingdoms" spoken of here will be nations as we know them. Some students of prophecy think that a ten-nation "United States of Europe" will emerge in the last days, and recent developments in Europe—the organization of the European Union and the use of the euro—seem to point in that direction. However, there are more than ten nations in the E.U., so we had better not draw hasty conclusions.[1] It is out of this confederation of ten nations, which in some way is an extension of the Roman Empire, that the Antichrist will come and the final world kingdom will be organized and actively oppose God and His people.

The "little horn" (vv. 8, 11, 24–26). This represents the last world ruler, the man called Antichrist. The Greek prefix *anti* can mean "against" and "instead of." The final world ruler will be both a counterfeit Christ and an enemy who is against Christ. John described the appearance of this "man of sin" (2 Thess. 2:3) in Revelation 13:1–10.[2] According to Daniel, the Antichrist has to overcome the power of three other rulers to be able to do what he wants to do and what Satan has planned for him to do (Dan. 7:24). The mention of his eyes suggests that he has remarkable knowledge and skill in planning his exploits. He will also be a man skilled in using words and able to promote himself so that people follow him (vv. 11, 25; Rev. 13:5–6). He will also blaspheme God and ultimately convince the unbelieving world that he is a god (2 Thess. 2:1–12). He will become the ruler of the world, and will control not only the economy and the religion, but also seek to change the times and the laws.

According to Daniel 7:25 and Revelation 13:5, his dictatorship will last for three and a half years, a significant period of time in the prophetic Scriptures. It's stated as "time, times and half a time" (Dan. 7:25 NIV; Rev. 12:14), "forty-two months" (11:2; 13:5) and "1,260 days" (11:3; 12:6).

This period is half of seven years, another significant time span in prophecy. We shall learn from Daniel 9:24–27 that the Antichrist will make a covenant with the Jewish nation for seven years, but in the midst of that period will break the covenant and begin to persecute God's people.

The scenario seems to look like this. Antichrist will be leading one of ten confederated nations in Europe. He will overcome three other nations and, with the help of Satan, move into becoming a world dictator. At first he will appear to be friendly to the Jews and will sign a seven-year covenant to protect them (v. 27).[3] The signing of that covenant is the signal for the start of the last seven years of Daniel's seventy weeks outlined in verses 24–27. This period is generally known as "the tribulation" and is described in Matthew 24:1–14; Mark 13:1–13; and Revelation 6—19.

After three and a half years, the Antichrist will break the covenant and set up his own image in the Jewish temple in Jerusalem, forcing the world to worship him and the Devil, who is energizing him. Using the language of Daniel, Jesus called this "the abomination of desolation" (Dan. 11:31; Matt. 24:15; Mark 13:14; 2 Thess. 2:1–4). This signals the last half of the tribulation, a period that is known as "the wrath of God" (Rev. 14:10, 19; 15:1, 7; and see Matt. 24:15–28; Mark 13:14–23). It will climax with the return of Jesus Christ to the earth and the defeat of Antichrist and his army (Matt. 24:29–44; Mark 13:24–27; Rev. 19:11–21). Jesus Christ will then establish His kingdom on earth (Dan. 7:13–14, 26–27; Rev. 20:1–6).[4]

Daniel doesn't go into all the details that John shares in the book of Revelation, but he does assure us that the kingdom of Satan and his counterfeit Christ will be defeated and destroyed by Jesus Christ (Dan. 7:22, 26; see 2 Thess. 1:6—2:10).

War on the saints (vv. 21–23, 25). The "saints" are mentioned in verses 18, 21–22, 25, and 27, and refer to the people of God living on the earth during the tribulation period. The apostle John makes it clear that there will be believing Jews and Gentiles on the earth during the seven years of the tribulation (Rev. 7). If the church is raptured before the tribulation, then these will be Jews and Gentiles who believe on Jesus Christ after the church departs. If the church goes through either part or all of the tribulation, then they will be the "saints" mentioned by Daniel. In either case, some of them will die for their faith (14:9–13).

Three of the texts describe the saints as victorious over their enemies (Dan. 7:18, 22, 27), while two texts inform us that the Lord permits them to be defeated before their enemies (vv. 21, 25). The saints "receive" the kingdom (not "take" as in v. 18), "possess" the kingdom (v. 22), and the kingdom is "given" to them (v. 27). All of this is the work of the Most High God. He permits Antichrist to rise to power and rule the world, and even allows him to make war on the saints and temporarily win the victory (v. 21). The phrase "wear out the saints" (v. 25) describes Antichrist's continual oppression of God's people and his blasphemous words against the Lord and His people.

John wrote the book of Revelation at a time when Rome was persecuting the church and trying to force Christians to worship the emperor. To confess "Jesus Christ is Lord" could mean imprisonment and even death. Both the book of Daniel and the book of Revelation brought encouragement and strength to the early church, just as they bring encouragement to suffering believers today.

THE KINGDOM OF CHRIST (7:9–14, 27–28)

Daniel has seen the rise and fall of five kingdoms: the Babylonians, the Medes and Persians, the Greeks, the Romans, and the kingdom of Satan headed by the Antichrist. But the most important kingdom of all is the kingdom that Christ shall establish on earth to the glory of God, the kingdom that Christians long for each time they pray, "Thy kingdom come"

(Matt. 6:10). Two aspects of the kingdom are seen in Scripture: "The kingdom of God," which is the spiritual reign of Christ over all who belong to Him (John 3:1–8; Col. 1:13) and the glorious kingdom on earth, prepared for God's people (Matt. 16:28; 25:34; 26:29; Luke 22:29).[5]

The heavenly throne of the Father (vv. 9–12). The thrones were put into place and not "cast down" as in the King James Version. This event takes place before the kingdom of Antichrist is destroyed, so it probably parallels Revelation 4—5, where John describes the throne room of God. "Ancient of days" (Dan. 7:9, 13, 22) is a name for God that emphasizes His eternality; He is the God who had existed from eternity past, has planned all things, and is working out His plan. The description of God must not be taken literally, because God doesn't have a body, wear clothes, or grow white hair. These things are symbolic of His nature and character: He is eternal, holy, and sovereign. In Revelation 1:12–20, these same characteristics are applied to Jesus Christ, thus proving that He is the eternal Son of God.

The vision of God's throne parallels Ezekiel 1:15–21, 26–27. The fire speaks of His holiness and judgment against sin and the wheels symbolize His providential working in the world in ways we can't understand. "Our God is a consuming fire" (Deut. 4:24; Heb. 12:29; see Ps. 97:1–4). He is praised by a multitude of saints and angels (Rev. 5:11) as the books are opened and the Lord prepares to judge evil on the earth. No matter what Satan and the Antichrist do on earth, God is still on the throne and He executes judgment.

The earthly throne of the Son of God (vv. 13–14, 27). "Son of Man" is a familiar title for our Lord Jesus Christ; it is used eighty-two times in the gospels, frequently by Jesus Himself. (See also Rev. 1:13; 14:14.) The phrase "clouds of heaven" reminds us of His promise to return in glory and reign on the earth (Matt. 24:30; 25:31; 26:64; Mark 13:26; 14:62; Rev. 1:7).

The Son of Man is presented before the throne of the Father and given dominion over all nations, an everlasting dominion that will never pass away. This is the prelude to the stone being cut out of the mountain and coming down to destroy the kingdoms of the world (Dan. 2:34–35, 44–45), and it parallels Revelation 5:1–7. The Father promised the Son, "Ask of Me, and I will give You the nations for Your inheritance, and the ends of the earth for Your possession" (Ps. 2:8 NKJV). Unlike the previous four kingdoms, and the kingdom of Antichrist, the kingdom of Jesus Christ can never be removed or destroyed. This is the kingdom that God had in mind when He told David that his throne would never end (2 Sam. 7:13, 16). He will share this kingdom with His people (Dan. 7:27) and they shall reign with Him (Rev. 5:10; 11:15; 20:4).

The kingdom covenant that God made with David (2 Sam. 7) will one day be fulfilled in Jesus Christ. God's promise that David's seed would have a throne and a kingdom forever (2 Sam. 7:12–13) was certainly not fulfilled in Solomon or any of his successors, but it will be fulfilled in Jesus Christ (Luke 1:30–33, 68–79).[6]

In Revelation 20:1–8, we are told six times that the kingdom will last for a thousand years, which is why it is called "the millennium," which is Latin for "thousand years." During that time, the Lord will fulfill the many kingdom promises made in the Old Testament Scriptures. Nature will be delivered from the bondage of sin and decay (Isa. 35; Rom. 8:18–25) and there will be peace in the world (Isa. 2:1–5; 9:1–7).

In this dramatic vision, Daniel had seen the vast sweep of history, beginning with the Babylonian kingdom and closing with the thousand-year reign of Christ on earth. What comfort and strength it must have given to him and to his people in exile that the prophecies would one day be fulfilled and their Messiah would reign on the throne of David. The church of Jesus Christ today looks for the Savior to return, and then we will be caught up to meet Him in the air (1 Thess. 4:13–18). We shall return with Him to earth, reign with Him, and serve Him. "Even so, come, Lord Jesus!" (Rev. 22:20 NKJV).

How did Daniel respond to this great revelation? He was deeply troubled and his face turned pale (Dan. 7:28 NIV), but he didn't tell anyone what the Lord had shown him. We shall learn in later chapters that after he had received a vision from the Lord, Daniel often became ill and was unable to work. This is quite unlike some "prophetic students" today who, when they think they've discovered a great truth, go on radio or television and tell everybody what they think they know. It's a dangerous thing to study prophecy just to satisfy our curiosity or to give people the impression that we are "great Bible students." If divine truth doesn't touch our own hearts and affect our conduct, then our Bible study is only an intellectual exercise to inflate our own ego.

Said A. W. Tozer: "The Bible doesn't approve of this modern curiosity that plays with the Scriptures and which seeks only to impress credulous and gullible audiences with the 'amazing' prophetic knowledge possessed by the brother who is preaching or teaching!"[7]

To this, I say a hearty "Amen!"

QUESTIONS FOR PERSONAL REFLECTION
OR GROUP DISCUSSION

1. When you think of a kingdom, what kind of images come to mind?

2. In Daniel's vision, nations are described as beasts. Describe the nations that are in the headlines today and the beasts that they most remind you of. *Russia - Bear, China dragon N Korea - Lion, Iran - a goat -*

3. What kinds of things do you see around you that remind you that the kingdom of Satan is still alive and well? *abortion, killing broken Marriages,*

4. When you think about the end times that Daniel's vision describes with the Antichrist and the world government, are you more afraid, intrigued, or excited? *Fearful*

5. List the traits of our current world climate that would enable a global leader like the Antichrist. *Money crisis, the virus, poverty, nuclear bombs*

6. What do you know about the tribulation? *7 years of trouble*

7. How do you think the churches of this nation will be affected when members begin to be martyred for their belief in God?

@ testing until

8. When God's kingdom is established, what are the things about our present world that you most look forward to being changed?

9. What do you think "peace in the world" will feel like?

10. Daniel's response to this prophecy was one of solemnity and sudden fright. What does Daniel's response tell you about him?

Chapter Eight

BEASTS, ANGELS, AND THE END TIMES

(Daniel 8)

From chapter 8 to the end of the book of Daniel, the text is written in Hebrew, for the major emphasis of these chapters is God's plan for the nation of Israel in the end times. From 2:4—7:28, the book is written in Aramaic because the emphasis in those chapters is on the Gentile kingdoms in history and prophecy. It was the nation of Israel that God chose to be the vehicle of His revelation and redemption in the world. Through the Jewish people came the knowledge of the one true and living God, the written Scriptures and, most important of all, the Savior, Jesus Christ. "Salvation is of the Jews" (John 4:22). In this chapter, five persons move across the great stage of prophecy and history.

1. DANIEL THE PROPHET (8:1–2, 15–19, 26–27)

King Belshazzar's third year was 551, so this vision came to Daniel before the fateful banquet described in chapter 5. This explains why the Babylonian Empire isn't mentioned, for within a dozen years Babylon would be taken by Cyrus, who would usher in the rule of the Medes and Persians. In terms of Nebuchadnezzar's great image (Dan. 2), the era of the head of gold would end and the era of the silver arms and chest would begin. The lion with the eagle's wings would be defeated by the bear with the ribs in its mouth (7:4–5).

Receiving the vision (vv. 1–2). Shushan (Susa) was a city about two hundred miles southeast of Babylon and at that time wasn't too important to the Babylonians. Eventually it became the capital of the Persian Empire (Neh. 1:1; Est. 1:2). The River Ulai (Dan. 8:2, 16) was probably a canal that flowed through Susa.

It's unlikely that Daniel left Babylon and traveled to Susa to receive the vision.[1] It's more likely that God transported him to Susa just as He transported Ezekiel to Jerusalem (Ezek. 8; 40) and the apostle John to the wilderness (Rev. 17:3) and to the high mountain (21:10). Since Daniel was about to describe the victory of the Medes and Persians over the Babylonians, God put him into the future capital of the Persian Empire.

Requesting the meaning of the vision (vv. 5–19). In the earlier part of the book, Daniel was able to interpret and explain the dreams and visions of others; but here he had to ask an angel for the meaning of the goat defeating the ram and the little horn becoming a mighty kingdom. The voice that commanded Gabriel may have been the voice of the Lord. Gabriel means "man of God," and it was he who explained to Daniel the vision given in chapter 8 as well as the vision about the seventy weeks (9:21–22). Centuries later, Gabriel would be sent to Zechariah to announce the birth of John the Baptist (Luke 1:11–20), and to Mary to announce that she would give birth to the Messiah (vv. 26–38). The only other angel who is named in Scripture is Michael ("Who is like God?"), who has been especially assigned to care for the nation of Israel (Dan. 10:13, 21; 12:1; Jude 9; Rev. 12:7).

When Gabriel moved closer to Daniel, the prophet became very frightened and fell into a faint and a deep sleep. (See Dan. 10:9, 15, 17.) Gabriel called him "son of man," which is a messianic title (Dan. 7:13); but here it was used to emphasize the weakness and humanness of the prophet. Gabriel's touch awakened Daniel (10:10–11, 16, 18), and the angel explained to him that the vision applied to the latter days of Jewish history. "The indignation" refers to God's displeasure with His people and the times of intense suffering Israel would endure before the coming of the end and the establishing of the promised kingdom.

2. Cyrus, King of Persia (8:3–4, 20)

This is the man who conquered Babylon. Centuries before Cyrus appeared on the scene, the prophet Isaiah called him by name and even called him God's "shepherd"[2] (Isa. 41:2, 25; 44:28—45:4). It was Cyrus whom God chose to defeat the Babylonians and permit the Jews to return to their land. Just as Babylon was identified with the lion and eagle, Persia was identified with the ram. The two horns symbolize the Medes and Persians, the Persians being the higher (stronger) of the two.

Cyrus and his armies did indeed "push westward and northward and southward" and defeat their enemies, taking Libya, Egypt, all of Asia Minor and moving as far as India, creating the largest empire ever in the ancient east until the time of Alexander the Great. Once his conquests were consolidated, he attacked Babylon and took it in 539. Cyrus was kind to those he took captive and permitted the Jews to return to their land to rebuild the temple and restore the nation (Isa. 44:28; 2 Chron. 36:22–23; Ezra 1:1–3; 6:2–5). He also allowed them to take with them the sacred vessels that Nebuchadnezzar had taken from the temple (Ezra 1:5–11).

The imagery used in connection with Cyrus is fascinating. He is called "the righteous man" (Isa. 41:2), or as the NIV puts it, "calling him in righteousness." This means that he was called to fulfill God's righteous purposes in freeing Israel from their Babylonian yoke and allowing them to return to their land. Our sovereign Lord can use even a pagan king to accomplish His purposes! Isaiah 41:25 pictures his victorious conquest as a man walking on mortar or on soft clay, because these materials can't resist him. The prophet Isaiah also called Cyrus the Lord's anointed (45:1) before whom He would go and open the way. Even the great gates of Babylon couldn't stand before his victorious march!

Why did God call Cyrus? "For the sake of Jacob my servant, of Israel my chosen" (v. 4 NIV). No matter how brutally the Gentile nations may treat the people of Israel, God uses the nations to accomplish His ordained purposes. His plans for Israel will be fulfilled no matter how much the Gentile nations may oppose His chosen people.

3. ALEXANDER THE GREAT OF GREECE (8:5–8, 21–22)

In Nebuchadnezzar's image, Greece was depicted as the thigh of brass (2:32, 39), and in Daniel's vision described in chapter 7, Greece was a swift leopard with four heads. Now Daniel sees Greece as an angry goat who runs so swiftly his feet don't even touch the ground! The large protruding horn represents Alexander the Great, who led the armies of Greece from victory to victory and extended his empire even beyond what Cyrus had done with the Persian army. But the horn was broken, for Alexander died in Babylon in June 323, at the age of thirty-three, and his vast kingdom was divided among four of his leaders, symbolized by the four horns that grew up (see 7:4–7; 11:4).

However, the remarkable conquests of Alexander were more than battle trophies, for they accomplished God's purposes in the world and helped to prepare the world for the coming of Christ and the spread of the gospel. For one thing, Alexander put an end to the Oriental influence that threatened to take over the Western world. At the same time, he "shook the ancient world to its very foundations" and "compelled the old world to think afresh."[3] By extending Greek culture and language, he helped to bring peoples together; and eventually the common (*koine*) Greek became the language of the New Testament. Even though his empire divided four ways after his death, Alexander brought nations together so they could interact with each other. His policy of kindness toward conquered peoples introduced a powerful example of brotherhood into the world. He literally "wedded East to West" when nine thousand of his soldiers and officers (some historians say ten thousand) married Eastern women in one mass wedding.

What Alexander and the Greeks began, the Romans completed, helping to prepare the ancient world for the coming of Christ. They are represented by the legs of iron (2:33, 40) and the "dreadful beast" (7:7). Roman roads and bridges enabled people to travel and share their ideas; Roman law kept nations under control; Roman legions enforced that law with an iron fist; and the Roman peace (*Pax Romana*) gave people the opportunity to experience more security than they had known before. All of this contributed to the taking of the Christian message throughout the Roman Empire, and sometimes, as in the case of Paul, Rome paid the bill for the missionaries to travel!

4. ANTIOCHUS IV EPIPHANES (8:9–14)[4]

As we have already seen, after the death of Alexander the Great (the "notable horn," v. 5), his empire was divided into four parts with four of his officers taking control (v. 8). Out of one of those horns a "little horn" appears who becomes a great leader, and this is Antiochus Epiphanes, the ruler of Syria from 175 to 163 BC and known as one of the cruelest tyrants in history.

Antiochus gave himself the name "Epiphanes," which means "illustrious, manifestation," for he claimed to be a revelation (epiphany) of the gods. He even had the word *theos* (god) put on the coins minted with his features on it, and his features on the coins came to look more and more like the Greek god Zeus. He had a passionate desire to turn the Jews into good Greeks. One of his first acts was to drive out the high priest Onias, an ardent Jew, and replace him with Jason, a patron of the Greeks. But Jason was replaced by Menelaus, who actually purchased the priesthood. Believing a rumor that the king was dead, Jason attacked Jerusalem only to learn that Antiochus was very much alive. The angry king attacked Jerusalem and plundered the temple. In 168 he sent an army of twenty thousand men under Apollonius to level Jerusalem. They entered the city on the Sabbath, murdered most of the men, and took the women and children as slaves. The remaining men fled to the army of the Jewish leader Judas Maccabeus.

But the king wasn't satisfied, so he issued an edict that there would be one religion in his realm and it wouldn't be the Jewish religion. He prohibited the Jews from honoring the Sabbath, practicing circumcision, and obeying the Levitical dietary laws, and he climaxed his campaign on December 14, 168, by replacing the Jewish altar with an altar to Zeus—and sacrificing a pig on it! Any Jew found possessing a copy of the law of Moses was slain. Jerusalem was eventually delivered by the courageous exploits of Judas Maccabeus and his followers, and on December 14, 165, the temple was purified, the altar of burnt offering restored, and Jewish worship once again restored. It is this event that the Jewish people celebrate as "The Feast of Lights" or Hanukkah (see John 10:22). Antiochus went mad while in Persia, where he died in 163.

Knowing these facts about Antiochus helps us better understand the text of Daniel's prophecy. Antiochus started in a small way but gradually accumulated power as he magnified himself and dealt ruthlessly with the Jewish people. He attacked the Jews in their "pleasant [beautiful]" land and put a stop to their religious practices. He even claimed that he was a god.

In verse 10, the Jews are described as "the host of heaven" (i.e., "godly people") and "stars" (Gen. 15:5; 22:17). When Antiochus stopped the daily sacrifices in the temple and substituted pagan worship, this was called "the abomination that makes desolate" ("the transgression of desolation," Dan. 8:13). This concept is found in 9:27; 11:31; and 12:11, and is used by Jesus in Matthew 24:15 and Mark 13:14. What Antiochus did was a foreshadowing of what the Antichrist will do when he puts his image in the temple and commands the world to worship him (2 Thess. 2; Rev. 13). Daniel 8:13 and 11:31 refer to Antiochus, and the other references to Antichrist, of whom Antiochus is a picture.

The two angels (8:13–14; "saints") spoke together about this matter, and from their conversation, Daniel learned the prophetic timetable. Between the desecration of the temple and its cleansing and restoration 2,300 days would pass. The Hebrew text reads "2,300 evenings and mornings," because burnt offerings were sacrificed at the temple each morning and each evening of every day. But does this mean 2,300 days or 1,150 days, 2,300 divided by two? And what date or event signals the beginning of the countdown? Some students opt for 2,300 days, that is, about six years, if you use 360 days for the year. Others prefer 1,150 days, which give us slightly over three years.

But what is the starting point for the countdown? The six-year advocates begin with 171 BC, when Antiochus deposed the true high priest. Subtract six years and this takes you to 165 when Judas Maccabeus defeated the enemy and reconsecrated the temple. However, the three-year advocates begin with the establishment of the pagan altar in the temple on 25 Kislev, 168, and this takes us to 165. Either approach meets the requirements of the prophecy.

We'll meet Antiochus Epiphanes again before we complete our study of the book of Daniel.

5. THE ANTICHRIST (8:23–27)

The angel awakened Daniel from his deep sleep and told him there was yet more prophetic truth for him to hear, and it related to "the time of wrath" (v. 19 NIV) and the "time of the end" (vv. 17, 19), which is the time of tribulation. The Old Testament prophets called this period "the time of Jacob's trouble" and "the day of the LORD," the period when God's wrath would be poured out on an evil world (Jer. 30:7; Isa. 2:11–12; 13:6, 9; Joel 2:1ff.; Zeph. 1). In other words, what Daniel learns in Daniel 8:23–27 relates to the end times when Antichrist will oppose God and God's people.

The "king of fierce countenance" is the Antichrist, not Antiochus Epiphanes; but if you compare verses 23–27 with verses 9–14, you will see that the characteristics and career of Antiochus parallel those of Antichrist.

- Both begin modestly but increase in power and influence.
- Both blaspheme God with mouths that speak great things.
- Both persecute the Jewish people.
- Both claim to be gods and put images in the temple.
- Both impose their own religion on the people.
- Both are opposed by a believing remnant that knows God.
- Both are energized by the Devil and are great deceivers.
- Both appear to succeed marvelously and seem to be invincible.
- Both are finally defeated by the coming of a redeemer (Judas Maccabeus and Jesus Christ).

Many other parallels exist, which you will discover as you study the relevant Scriptures.

The "Prince of princes" (v. 25) is Jesus Christ, who is also the "God of gods" (11:36) and the "KING OF KINGS" (Rev. 19:16). Antichrist opposes Jesus Christ and seeks to replace Him, but ultimately Jesus Christ defeats Antichrist and consigns him, his false prophet, and Satan to the lake of fire (20:1–3).

As a result of this experience of receiving the vision and communing with angels, Daniel became ill. One cause of his physical and emotional collapse was his inability to understand where this vision of the "king of fierce countenance," prefigured by "the little horn," fit into the prophetic scheme for Israel. He knew that the "little horn" would appear in the last days, but what would occur between his day and that day? He would learn from Jeremiah's prophecy that his people would be released from bondage and allowed to return to their land and rebuild their temple, but Daniel knew nothing about God's "mystery" concerning the church (Eph. 3:1–13) or the "mystery" concerning the partial blinding and hardening of Israel (Rom. 11:25–36). And who was the "king of fierce countenance" and why would he attack the Jewish people? Daniel felt the burden of the suffering his people would experience, and he knew the awful consequences of truth being cast to the ground (Dan. 8:12; Isa. 59:14–15).

Daniel is a good example for students of prophecy to follow. He asked the Lord for the explanation (Dan. 8:15) and allowed the Lord to instruct him. But his investigation into God's prophetic program wasn't a matter of satisfying curiosity or trying to appear very knowledgeable before others. He was concerned about his people and the work they had to do on earth. He so identified with what he learned that it made him ill! Too many "prophetic students" don't wait before God for instruction and insight, nor do they feel burdened when they learn God's truth about the future. Instead, they try to display their "knowledge" and impress people with what they think they know. The whole exercise is purely academic; it's all in the head and never changes the hearts.

When he got over his weakness and sickness, the prophet went back to work for the king and didn't tell anybody what he had learned. But God still had more truth to teach him, and he was ready to receive it.

QUESTIONS FOR PERSONAL REFLECTION
OR GROUP DISCUSSION

1. Why do you think God spoke so often in visions in Daniel's time but
not today? *God spoke in visions to communicate*
Today God's word is written down.

2. Who are the people in our culture who speak with the credibility and
stature that Daniel did? *People who speak with credibility are*
People who know the Word

3. Name some people in politics who, like Cyrus, have been used by God
even though they were unaware of it.
Chuck Colson

4. In what ways have you seen God care for His people through political
forces?

5. Who would you say are the top five people, including Alexander the
Great, who have shaped the world as we know it? *Jesus Christ, Martin Luther, John Wesley*
Abraham Lincoln, Billy Graham

6. How do you think history would have played itself out differently if
Alexander had not "put an end to the Oriental influence that threatened
to take over the Western world"?

7. If Antiochus was one of the top five cruelest tyrants in history, who would be the other four?

Nero, Hitler, Mao Stalin, Ivan the [terrible]
Genghis Kahn

8. If you had been Jewish at the time when Antiochus outlawed everything that had to do with the Jewish culture, what would you have done to preserve that culture underground?

Put writings in clay pots

9. In what ways do you think Christians will recognize the Antichrist when he comes to power?

We will recognize the Antichrist by his rejection of Christ

10. If Daniel's response to the threats at the end of the world was grim, what do you think our response should be?

Our lives need to be holy

Chapter Nine

THE PROPHETIC CALENDAR

(Daniel 9)

When speaking at a press conference in Cairo on February 1, 1943, Sir Winston Churchill said, "I always avoid prophesying beforehand, because it is a much better policy to prophesy after the event has already taken place."

Among the Jewish people, that kind of "prophetic" activity could have resulted in the death of the so-called prophet (Deut. 18:20–22). Worshipping false gods and listening to false prophets had led to Israel's spiritual decay and ultimate collapse as a nation. The people hadn't obeyed what the prophets commanded, so Israel was exiled in Babylon; and there they learned to take the prophetic word very seriously, because it was the only hope they possessed. The church today needs to heed the word of prophecy because it's the light of certainty in a world of darkness and uncertainty (2 Peter 1:19–21).

Note three stages in Daniel's experience with the prophetic message that spoke concerning his people and the city of Jerusalem.

1. INSIGHT: LEARNING GOD'S PLAN (9:1–2)

The first year of Darius was 539 BC, the year that Babylon fell to the Medes and the Persians.[1] This great victory was no surprise to Daniel, because God had already told him that the Medo-Persian Empire would conquer Babylon. In Nebuchadnezzar's great "dream image," the head of gold would be replaced by the chest and arms of silver (chap. 2); and later visions revealed that the bear would conquer the lion (chap. 7). But long before Daniel's day, both Isaiah and Jeremiah had predicted the fall of Babylon, so it's no surprise that Daniel started studying afresh the scroll of the prophet Jeremiah.

The Word of God. One of the beautiful things about the inspired Word of God is its constant freshness; no matter how often we read it, there is always something new to learn or something familiar to see in a new light. Had Jeremiah's scrolls of the Old Testament been organized like our modern Bibles, he would have read Jeremiah 24 and been reassured that the Lord would care for His people no matter what ruler was on the throne. From 25:1–14, he would learn the reason for the exile as well as the length of the exile—seventy years—and this would be corroborated in 29:10–14. The exile of the Jews in Babylon was no accident; it was a divine appointment, and they would not be released until the very time that God had ordained.

Daniel called Jeremiah's writings "the word of the LORD." King Jehoiakim had tried to burn up Jeremiah's prophecies, but the Lord preserved them because they were His very words (Jer. 36). "Heaven and earth will pass away, but my words will never pass away" (Matt. 24:35 NIV). "The grass withers and the flowers fall, but the word of our God stands forever" (Isa. 40:8 NIV). "Long ago I learned from your statutes that you established them to last forever" (Ps. 119:152 NIV). Over the centuries, people have ignored, denied, attacked, and sought to destroy the Holy Scriptures, but the Word of God is still here! God especially protected the scrolls written by Jeremiah because He wanted Daniel to have a copy to take with him to Babylon.

"All scripture is given by inspiration of God" (2 Tim. 3:16), the Old Testament as well as the New, and Holy Scripture is the only dependable source of truth about God, man, sin, salvation, and the future events God has in His great plan. In these days of rapidly changing ideas, events, and situations, the unchanging Word of God is our dependable light and unshakable foundation.

The God of the Word. This is the first time that Jehovah, the covenant name of God, is used in the book of Daniel, and it is used only in this chapter (vv. 2–3, 10, 13–14, 20). But we must remember that, at that time, the Lord was calling the nation of Israel "Lo-Ruhama—not loved" and "Lo-Ammi—not my people" (Hos. 1) because Israel had broken His holy covenant. When you are outside the covenant, you can't sincerely use His covenant name and expect to receive covenant blessings.

However, Daniel came to God pleading for mercy and forgiveness for himself and his people, and that's the kind of praying the Lord Jehovah wants to hear. In fact, the promise of God's forgiveness was written right into the covenant. "But if they confess their iniquity and the iniquity of their fathers, with their unfaithfulness in which they were unfaithful to Me, and that they also have walked contrary to Me … then I will remember My covenant with Jacob, and My covenant with Isaac and My covenant with Abraham I will remember; I will remember the land" (Lev. 26:40, 42 NKJV). Certainly as Daniel studied the Scriptures and prayed to Jehovah, he had in his mind and heart both the holy covenant (Lev. 26; Deut. 27—28) and Solomon's prayer at the dedication of the temple (1 Kings 8:33–36).

God's plan for His people. God revealed to Jeremiah that the people of Israel would be taken to Babylon and be exiled from their land for seventy years (Jer. 25:11–12; 29:10). God had commanded His people to give the land a "sabbath rest" every seven years and a "Year of Jubilee" every fifty years (Lev. 25). Both the forty-ninth and the fiftieth years would be "sabbatic years" when the people were not allowed to sow seed or cultivate their orchards. They had to trust God to make the food grow to meet their daily needs. This law was not only good for the land, helping to restore its fertility, but it was also good for the spiritual life of the nation. However, it was not until the nation's captivity in Babylon that the land enjoyed its sabbath rests (2 Chron. 36:20–21).

From what date do we begin to count off the seventy years, and when did the captivity officially end? To answer these important questions, we must highlight the key dates in Jewish history at that time. Babylon began to attack the kingdom of Judah in 606 BC, and Jerusalem and the temple were destroyed in 586. The first Jewish captives were taken to Babylon in 605, Daniel and his three friends being among them. In 538, Cyrus issued the decree that permitted the Jews to return to their land and rebuild the temple (Ezra 1:1–4), and in 537 about fifty thousand Jews returned to Jerusalem under the leadership of Zerubbabel and Joshua the high priest (Ezra 1—2).

If we decide that the captivity officially began in 606–605 with the attack on Jerusalem and the deporting of the first captives, then seventy years later would take us to 537–536, when the first exiles returned to their land and the foundations of the temple were laid. In other words, the first captives left Judah in 605 and the liberated exiles returned to the land in 537–36, a time period of roughly seventy years. However, some students feel that the destruction of Jerusalem and the temple should be the starting point (586), with the captivity not officially ending until the second temple had been built and dedicated (515), another period of approximately seventy years. Since both interpretations make sense, it shouldn't be necessary to debate the issue.

We need to be aware of three important facts. First, in sending His people into captivity, the Lord was keeping His covenant promise, for He had warned them that they would be punished if they persisted in disobeying Him (Lev. 26). It appears that Israel's years of captivity in Babylon helped to cure the Jewish people of their detestable sin of idol worship.

Second, the captivity brought blessing to the land, for the land had been abused by farmers who would not let the land enjoy its sabbatical rests. The land belonged to the Lord (25:23; see Deut. 11:12), and He would not permit His people to defile it by sin and idolatry and waste it by not giving it times of rest. For every sabbatical year the Jews failed to honor, they added one more year to their own bondage in Babylon.

Third, when Daniel made this discovery about the seventy years, the period of captivity was about to end! If Daniel was taken to Babylon in 605, and he discovered Jeremiah's prophecy in 539, then he had been in Babylon sixty-six or sixty-seven years. The next year (538), Cyrus would make his decree permitting the Jews to return to their land. The prophet was probably eighty-one years old at this time. He himself would not be able to return to the land, but he rejoiced that others could return.

2. Intercession: Praying for God's Mercy (9:3–19)

Daniel is a wonderful example of balance in the spiritual life, for he devoted himself to both the Word of God and prayer (Acts 6:4). Some believers are so wrapped up in prophetic studies that they have little concern for the practical outworking of God's will. All they want to do is satisfy their curiosity and then proudly share their "insights" with others. When Daniel learned God's truth, the experience humbled him and moved him to worship and to pray.

Preparing for prayer (v. 3). You don't have to read very far in the book of Daniel before you discover that he was a man of prayer. Daniel and his three friends sought the face of God when Nebuchadnezzar threatened to slay all the magicians and counselors (2:16–23). It was Daniel's habit to pray to the Lord three times each day (6:10–11), a practice he continued even when it was illegal to pray to anyone except the king. When God showed Daniel visions of future events, the prophet wasn't satisfied until he had asked for an explanation (7:15ff.; 8:15ff.). Prayer was a vital part of Daniel's life.

Daniel prepared himself to pray, because he knew that his prayer would affect the future of the Jewish nation and the lives of the Jewish captives in Babylon. It would be his holy task to confess the sins of the Jewish nation, asking God to forgive His people and receive them back again. He humbled himself in sackcloth and ashes; he fasted; and he directed his heart and mind to the Lord. Preparation for prayer and worship is as important as prayer itself, for without a heart that is right with God, our prayers are just so many pious words. Daniel met the conditions for answered prayer set forth in Leviticus 26:40–45 and 2 Chronicles 7:14.

Worshipping the Lord (v. 4). Too often we rush into God's presence and ask for things, without first pausing to worship Him. Daniel prepared himself for prayer, as did Ezra (Ezra 9:3–5) and the Levites (Neh. 9:5–6). It's important that we focus on the character of God and not become too preoccupied with ourselves and our burdens. The "invocation" to Daniel's prayer is a primer of biblical theology. His words describe a God who is great and faithful to keep His promises, a God who loves His people and gives them His Word to obey so that He can bless them. He is a merciful God (Dan. 9:18) who forgives the sins of His people when they come to Him in contrition and confession.[2] This is also the way Nehemiah prayed when he sought God's will concerning rebuilding the walls of Jerusalem (Neh. 1:5ff.).

It's one thing to pray to the Lord and quite something else to be a worshipping intercessor. When we see the greatness and glory of God, it helps to put our own burdens and needs in proper perspective. By exercising even little faith in a great God, we can move the hand of God to accomplish wonders that will glorify His name. Dr. Robert A. Cook used to say, "If you can explain what's going on in your ministry, God didn't do it."

Confessing sin (vv. 5–15). Several times in Israel's ministry, the intercession of one person brought about the nation's deliverance from judgment. On two occasions, God was ready to wipe out the entire Jewish nation, but the intercession of Moses stayed His hand (Ex. 32:7–14; Num. 14:10–25). God answered Elijah's prayer and sent the rain that was so desperately needed (1 Kings 18), and He heard Jehoshaphat's prayer and gave Israel victory over the large invading army of Moabites and Ammonites (2 Chron. 20). King Hezekiah cried out to God when the Assyrian army surrounded Jerusalem, and the Lord sent His angel to slay 185,000 enemy soldiers (Isa. 37; 2 Kings 19). "The prayer of a righteous man is powerful and effective" (James 5:16 NIV). God doesn't have to wait for the entire nation to repent and cry out for mercy; He will start to work when He hears the believing prayers of one faithful intercessor.

While Daniel's prayer was certainly personal, he so identified with the people of Israel that his prayer involved national concerns. The pronoun he uses is "we" rather than "they" or "I." He confessed that he and the people had sinned greatly against the Lord and broken the terms of His gracious covenant. According to Daniel 9:5–6, the Jews had sinned, rebelled, turned away from His law, disobeyed His commands, done wrong, and refused to listen to the messengers God had sent to them. "And the LORD God of their fathers sent warnings to them by His messengers, rising up early and sending them, because He had compassion on His people and on His dwelling place. But they mocked the messengers of God, despised His words, and scoffed at His prophets, until the wrath of the LORD arose against His people, till there was no remedy" (2 Chron. 36:15–16 NKJV). God had been longsuffering with His covenant people, but the time came when He had to act.

What were the consequences of the nation's rebellion? They became a sinful people, a people covered with shame ("confusion of face," Dan. 9:8), and a scattered people. Their land was overrun by enemy soldiers, their great city of Jerusalem was destroyed, and their holy temple was desecrated, robbed, and burned. No wonder the Jews were ashamed! But it was their own sins that had brought these disasters, because their kings, princes, and priests had disobeyed God's laws and refused to obey God's prophets.

The leaders and the people knew the terms of God's covenant, but they deliberately violated them. The Jews were unfaithful to God's covenant, but God was faithful to keep His word. If the nation had obeyed, God would have been faithful to bless them (Ps. 81:11–16); but because they rebelled, He was faithful to chasten them. "You have fulfilled the words spoken against us and against our rulers by bringing upon us great disaster" (Dan. 9:12 NIV). Daniel didn't make excuses for the nation, nor did he say that God's covenant was too demanding. Israel had enjoyed great blessings when they had obeyed the law, so why should they complain when they experienced great suffering because they disobeyed the law?

But there was something even worse than the sins that brought divine punishment to Israel. It was the refusal of the Jews to repent and confess their sins even after being taken captive! They spent their time praying for judgment against Babylon (Ps. 137) rather than seeking God's face and asking for His forgiveness. God's will for Israel in captivity was outlined in Jeremiah 29, but the Jews didn't always follow it. Daniel's approach was biblical: "For the LORD our God is righteous in everything he does" (Dan. 9:14 NIV). Why would He bring His people out of Egypt and then allow them to waste away in Babylon? Daniel knew that God had purposes for Israel to fulfill, and so he reminded God of His past mercies (v. 15).

Asking for mercy on Israel (vv. 16–19). God in His grace gives us what we don't deserve, and God in His mercy doesn't give us what we do deserve. Daniel asked the Lord to turn away His anger from Jerusalem and the holy temple. He admitted that the sins of Israel (including Daniel) were the cause of that great catastrophe, but that God had promised to forgive if His people would repent and confess their sins. "We do not make requests of you because we are righteous, but because of your great mercy" (v. 18 NIV). But even more, Daniel desired the nation to be restored that God might be glorified. After all, the Jews were God's chosen people, and Jerusalem was the place of His holy temple; the longer the people and the land were under God's wrath, the less glory the Lord would receive. "Your city and your people bear your Name" (v. 19 NIV).[3]

God answered Daniel's prayer. The next year, Cyrus issued a decree that permitted the Jews to return to their land, take the temple treasures with them, rebuild the temple, and restore the worship. What a remarkable ministry Daniel had in Babylon! He was counselor to four kings, intercessor for the people of Israel, a faithful witness to the true and living God, and the author of one of the basic books of prophecy in the Old Testament.

Daniel now knew God's immediate plans for the nation of Israel, but what about the distant future? He had already learned from the visions God gave him that difficult days lay ahead for God's people, with a kingdom to appear that would crush everything good and promote everything evil. Would God's people survive? Would the promised Messiah finally appear? Would the kingdom of God be established on the earth?

Daniel is about to receive the answers to those questions.

3. INSTRUCTION: DISCOVERING GOD'S TIMETABLE (9:20–27)

We don't know at what time of day Daniel began to pray, but he was still praying at the time of the evening burnt offering, which was about three o'clock in the afternoon. He was living in Babylon but was still measuring time by Jewish religious practices! His body was in Babylon, but his mind and heart were in Jerusalem. Had the temple been standing and the priests still officiating, this would have been "the ninth hour," when the lamb was offered as a burnt offering (Ex. 29:38–41; Acts 3:1; 10:30). It was one of the three occasions during the day when Daniel set aside time to offer special prayer to the Lord (Dan. 6:10; Ps. 55:17). This was also the time when Ezra the scribe prayed for God to forgive the sins of the Jewish remnant that had returned to the land (Ezra 9:5). There is a sense in which prayer is seen by God as a spiritual sacrifice to Him (Ps. 141:1–2).

While Daniel was praying, the angel Gabriel came swiftly to him, interrupted his prayer, touched him, and spoke to him. Daniel had met Gabriel after seeing the vision of the ram and the goat, and Gabriel had explained its meaning to him (Dan. 8:15ff.). Now the angel had come to explain to Daniel what God had planned for Jerusalem, the temple, and the Jewish people. The phrase "fly swiftly" (9:21) has given rise to the idea that angels have wings and fly from place to place, but arrows, bullets, and missiles fly swiftly and don't have wings. Angels are spirits and therefore don't have bodies (Ps. 104:4; Heb. 1:7). When they appear to humans, they take on temporary human form. The angelic creatures seen by Isaiah (Isa. 6:2) and Ezekiel (Ezek. 1:6, 8, 11) did have wings, but they were special creatures performing special ministries. The NIV translates the phrase "in swift flight" (Dan. 9:21) and makes no mention of wings.

The seventy "weeks" (v. 24). The word *weeks* means "sevens," so Gabriel was speaking about seventy periods of 7 years, or 490 years. Keep in mind that these years relate specifically to Daniel's people, the Jews, and their Holy City, Jerusalem. In his prayer, Daniel's great concern was that his people be forgiven their sins against the Lord, the city be rebuilt, and the temple be restored (v. 16); and these are the matters that Gabriel will discuss. To apply this important prophecy to any other people or place is to rob it of its intended meaning.

Gabriel explained that during those 490 years, the Lord would accomplish six specific purposes for the Jewish people. The first three have to do with sin and the last three with righteousness. The Lord would "finish the transgression," that is, the transgression of the Jewish people, and "make an end of" Israel's national sins. This was one of the main burdens of Daniel's prayer. Israel was a scattered suffering nation because she was a sinful nation. How would the Lord accomplish this? By making "reconciliation for iniquity," that is, by offering a sacrifice that would atone for their sin. Here we come to the cross of Jesus Christ, Israel's Messiah.

When Jesus died on the cross, He died for the sins of the whole world (1 John 2:2; John 1:29), and therefore we can proclaim the good news of the gospel to sinners everywhere. But He also died for the church (Eph. 5:25) and for the people of Israel. "For the transgression of my people was he stricken" (Isa. 53:8). Jesus died for sinners in every tribe and nation (Rev. 5:9; 7:9), but in a very special way, He died for His own people, the Jewish nation (John 11:44–52).

The last three divine purposes focus on righteousness and the future kingdom of Messiah. When Jesus returns, He will establish His righteous kingdom (Jer. 23:5–6; 31:31–34) and rule in righteousness (Isa. 4:2–6). In that day, the Old Testament prophecies of Israel's glorious kingdom will be fulfilled, and there will be no need for visions or prophets. "To anoint the most Holy" refers to the sanctifying of the future temple that is described in Ezekiel 40—48.

These six purposes declare the answers to Daniel's prayer! Ultimately, Israel's sins will be forgiven (Zech. 12:10—13:1), the city of Jerusalem will be rebuilt, and the temple and its ministry will be restored, all because of the atoning death of Jesus Christ on the cross. All of these wonderful accomplishments will be fulfilled during the 490 years that Gabriel goes on to explain. He divides the seven sevens—490 years—into three significant periods: 49 years, 434 years, and 7 years.[4]

First period—49 years (v. 25). During this period, the Jews will rebuild the city of Jerusalem in troubled times. The key issue here is the date of the decree. This is not the decree of Cyrus in 538 permitting the Jews to return to their land and rebuild their temple (Ezra 1; Isa. 44:28), because the emphasis of this decree is on the city of Jerusalem. While some students opt for the decree of Artaxerxes in 457, sending Ezra to Jerusalem (Ezra 7:12–26), that decree also emphasized the temple and its ministry. The decree of Daniel 9:25 is probably that of Artaxerxes in 445 authorizing Nehemiah to go to Jerusalem to rebuild the walls and restore the gates (Neh. 2:5–8).

Second period—434 years (v. 26). Gabriel affirmed that 483 years are involved from the giving of the decree to the coming of "the Anointed One, the ruler" (7 x 7 = 49; 7 x 62 = 434; total = 483). When you count 483 solar years from the year 445, you end up with AD 29/30, which brings us to the time of Christ's ministry on earth.[5] But this Anointed One, the Christ, will not be permitted to rule; for His people cried out, "We have no king but Caesar" (John 19:15). "We will not have this man to reign over us" (Luke 19:14). The Messiah will be "cut off, but not for himself" ("and will have nothing," NIV). This speaks of His rejection by the Jewish nation (John 1:11; Luke 13:33–35) and His crucifixion as a criminal, turned over to the Roman authorities by His own people and one of His own disciples. But He died for the sins of the world, including the sins of the Jewish nation.

We know that Jesus arose from the dead and returned to heaven. He sent the Holy Spirit to empower His people to bear witness to the whole world (Acts 1:8), beginning in Jerusalem (Luke 24:46–53). But the same nation that allowed John the Baptist to be slain and asked for Jesus to be crucified went on to persecute the church and themselves kill Stephen (Acts 7). In AD 70, the prophecy in Daniel 9:26 was fulfilled when the Roman armies destroyed Jerusalem and the temple, and the Jewish nation was scattered. The Romans are "the people of the prince that shall come," and that prince is the future Antichrist that Daniel described as "the little horn" and the blasphemous king (7:8, 24–25; 8:23–27). This takes us to the third period.

Third period—7 years (v. 27). The pronoun "he" refers to "the prince that shall come" (v. 26), this is the Antichrist.[6] We are now in the final seven years of the prophetic calendar that Gabriel gave Daniel, the period that we know as "the tribulation" or "the day of the LORD." While the world has always known wars and desolations (Matt. 24:3–24), the end of the age will introduce a time of terrible suffering that will climax with the return of Jesus Christ (Rev. 6—19; Matt. 24:15–35).

The event that triggers this last seven-year period is the signing of a covenant between the Antichrist and the Jewish nation. At this time, the Antichrist is a key political figure in Europe—one of the ten toes of the image in Daniel 2, and the "little horn" who emerges from the ten horns in 7:8, 24ff.—and he has the authority and ability to end the "Middle East problem." He covenants to protect the Jews from their enemies, probably so they can build their temple and restore their sacrifices. The spiritually blind Jewish leaders, ignorant of their own Scriptures, will gladly enter into the covenant. "I have come in My Father's name, and you do not receive Me," Jesus told the Jewish leaders of His day; "if another comes in his own name, him you will receive" (John 5:43 NKJV).

After three and a half years, the Antichrist will break the covenant, seize the temple, and put his own image there, and will force the world to worship him (2 Thess. 2; Rev. 13). This is the "abomination of desolation" (Dan. 11:31; 12:11 NKJV) that Jesus spoke about that marks the midpoint of the tribulation period (Matt. 24:15; Mark 13:14). The "man of sin" and "son of perdition" (2 Thess. 2:3), who up till now has deceived the world by playing a shrewd political game, will now reveal himself as a tool of Satan and a cruel world dictator. Christ will defeat him when He returns to establish His kingdom (Rev. 19:11–21).

The strange parenthesis. Whether Daniel understood all that he heard is not revealed to us, but Gabriel's message assured him that the nation of Israel would be restored to their land, the city of Jerusalem and the temple would be rebuilt, and God would make provision for the cleansing of the nation. But Gabriel didn't tell Daniel what would happen between the sixty-ninth and the seventieth "weeks." Between Daniel 9:26 and 27 there is a strange parenthesis. Why?

Because this prophecy has to do with the Jews, the Jewish temple, and the city of Jerusalem (v. 24). But the period of time between the sixty-ninth and seventieth weeks has to do with the church, the body of Christ, which was a mystery God had hidden in Old Testament times and didn't reveal until the time of Christ and the apostles (Eph. 3:1–13).[7] Daniel wasn't told that the rejection and death of the Messiah would bring about a new thing, a spiritual body that would include Jews and Gentiles and in which all natural differences would be unimportant (Eph. 2:11–22; Gal. 3:22–29). One reason the Jewish legalists opposed Paul was because he put Jews and Gentiles on the same level in the church, and the traditionalists wanted to maintain the "superiority" of the Jews as revealed in the law and the kingdom prophecies.

Some of the prophecy in Daniel 9:24–27 has already been fulfilled, and the rest will be fulfilled in the end times. We are today living in the age of the church, when Israel has been partially blinded and temporarily set aside (Rom. 9—11). Like Paul, we must have a heart concern for the Jewish people, pray for them, and seek to share the gospel with them. Gentile believers have a debt to the people of Israel (Rom. 15:24–27) because they gave us the knowledge of the true and living God, the inspired written Scriptures, and the Savior, Jesus Christ.

The Lord still has more to teach Daniel about the future of His people, and we will consider these prophecies in the chapters to come.

QUESTIONS FOR PERSONAL REFLECTION
OR GROUP DISCUSSION

1. In Daniel's day the hope of the Jews was getting back to their home-
   land. How would you describe the hope of Christians today?

   The immediate hope of today's Christians is to live a faithful life for Jesus, + be ready for Christ's return.

2. When Babylon fell, Daniel turned back to the prophecies. What part
   of God's Word do you turn to when you need to get your balance in the
   midst of transition?

   When I need balancing I seek God's message in all of scripture.

   2 Chron 7:14; Phil 4:14

3. Daniel saw prophecy fulfilled before his eyes. From your experiences of
   seeing the promises of God's Word come to life, how do you think that
   affected Daniel?

   I believe Daniel was encouraged as he saw scriptures coming into action & reality.

4. Why do you think people today sometimes get so wrapped up in
   prophecy that it almost becomes an end unto itself?

   Prophecy can take away from the gospel and lead to Rapidism

5. Daniel prepared himself for prayer. What kinds of preparations do you
   think we could use to make our prayers more effective, not only in getting answers, but also in changing us?

   Pray the ACTS of prayer. Praise, Confession, Thanksgiving + Supplication

6. Dr. Robert Cook said, "If you can explain what's going on in your ministry, God didn't do it." What does that have to say to us about our prayer life? *If the pattern of prayer is the importante part we may loose the ext aspect of Love exchange.*

7. What kinds of things keep us from confessing our sins, as individuals and as a nation? *Our pride keeps individuals & nations from confessing our need of help*

8. In what ways do our confession and repentance free God's work in our lives? *God cannot work with a proud heart which seeks to resist Him.*

9. What fears do you think Daniel would have had in hearing about the destruction that was to come? *Daniel trusted in God's mercy*

10. What fears do you have as you think about the end of the world as we know it? *Love cast out fear*

Chapter Ten

A REMARKABLE
EXPERIENCE
(Daniel 10)

The third year of Cyrus would be 536 BC, which is the latest date given in the book of Daniel. This statement doesn't contradict 1:21, which tells us how long Daniel continued in the king's court. As we have seen, Daniel lived long enough to see Jeremiah's prophecy fulfilled and the first group of Jewish exiles return to their land and start to rebuild the temple. If he was fifteen when he was taken to Babylon, then he would be eighty-four or eighty-five at this time.

The fact that 10:1 speaks of Daniel in the third person suggests that the statement that opens this chapter may be an official "identification title" for the last three chapters of his book. In verse 2 and throughout the chapter, Daniel speaks in the first person. Also, the use of his Babylonian name, "Belteshazzar," indicates that this opening statement is probably an official "label" for the document. The vision God showed him was true, and Daniel understood the message of the vision and realized that it would be fulfilled many years later. The phrase "the time appointed was long" can also be translated "and of great conflict" (NIV, "and it concerned a great war"). Daniel would learn that his people would experience great suffering in the years ahead, but that the Lord would watch over them and ultimately establish the promised kingdom.

A CONCERNED PROPHET (10:1–3)

For three weeks, Daniel had fasted and prayed and used no ointments as he sought the face of the Lord. Why? One reason was probably his concern for the nearly fifty thousand Jews who a year before had left Babylon and traveled to their native land to rebuild the temple. Since Daniel had access to official reports, he no doubt heard that the remnant had arrived safely in Jerusalem and that all of the tabernacle treasures were intact. He also would have heard that the men had laid the foundation of the temple but that the work had been opposed and finally stopped (Ezra 4). He knew that his people were suffering hardship in the ruined city of Jerusalem, and he wondered if God would fail to fulfill the promises He made to Jeremiah (Jer. 25:11–12; 29:10–14).

Daniel may not have understood that the prophecy of the seventy years had a dual application, first to the people and then to the temple. The first Jews were deported to Babylon in 605, and the first captives returned to their land in 536, a period of seventy years. The temple was destroyed in 586 by the Babylonian army, and the second temple was completed and dedicated in 515, another period of seventy years. Daniel was burdened that the house of God be rebuilt as quickly as possible, but he didn't realize that God was fulfilling His plans without a mistake. The work was stopped in 536, it resumed 520 and it was completed in 515. That sixteen-year delay kept everything right on schedule. This is a good reminder to us as we serve the Lord today, that our times are in His hands (Ps. 31:15) and He is never late in accomplishing His will.

But there may have been a second reason why Daniel was fasting and praying: He wanted to understand more about the visions and prophecies he had already received, and he longed for the Lord to reveal additional truth to him about the future of Israel. Daniel was an aged man, and before he went to his grave, he wanted to leave behind a prophetic message that would encourage and strengthen his people. Doubtless the prophecy of Daniel was a treasured book to the people of Israel in the centuries that followed. They knew they would experience great trials and persecutions, and yet they also knew that the Lord would be faithful and that they would one day enter into the promised kingdom.

When one day we gather in heaven, we will discover that what happened to God's people on earth depended a great deal on the prayers of burdened people like Daniel. "For who will have pity on you, O Jerusalem? Or who will bemoan you? Or who will turn aside to ask how you are doing?" (Jer. 15:5 NKJV). Nehemiah asked about the plight of Jerusalem and ended up being an answer to his own prayers (Neh. 1—2)! Jeremiah wept over Jerusalem and its people and wished that he could have wept more (Jer. 9:1–2; 8:21; 10:19; 23:9). Jesus also wept over the city (Matt. 23:37–39), and the apostle Paul was willing to be condemned himself that his people might be saved (Rom. 9:1–3; 10:1). "Rivers of tears gush from my eyes because people disobey your instructions" (Ps. 119:136 NLT).

God laid a burden on Daniel's heart, and because Daniel fasted and prayed, we are studying his prophecies today. May the Lord help us to leave something behind in the journey of life so that those who come after us will be encouraged and helped!

AN AWESOME VISION (10:4–9, 14)

Three days after the end of his fast, Daniel saw an awesome vision as he stood by the Tigris River. Why Daniel was there isn't explained in the text, but it was the place where God met with him and revealed Israel's future in the greatest prophecy God ever gave to His servant.

It was during the first month of the Hebrew year that the Jews celebrated Passover, the Feast of Unleavened Bread, and the Feast of Firstfruits (Lev. 23:1–14). Daniel couldn't celebrate these special events in Babylon, but certainly his heart was meditating on them. Passover spoke of Israel's release from Egyptian bondage, and now the Jews were being permitted to leave Babylon for their own land. During the week before Passover, the Jews had to remove every bit of leaven from their houses, a picture of sin being put out of their lives (Matt. 16:6–12; Mark 8:15; Luke 12:1; 1 Cor. 5:6–8; Gal. 5:9). Though he lived for eight decades in a pagan land, Daniel had kept his heart and life pure before God. He was praying that the Jewish remnant living in Jerusalem would be a holy people to the Lord so that He could bless them in their work.

Suddenly, without announcement, Daniel saw an awesome sight: a man wearing a linen garment and a golden girdle, with a body like chrysolite (topaz) and a face like lightning, his eyes like flaming torches, his arms and feet gleaming like polished brass, and his voice sounding like a great multitude. We aren't told what the man said when he spoke, but the combination of his appearance and his speech was overwhelming. The men with Daniel didn't see the vision, but they felt the terror of a powerful presence and hid themselves.[1] Daniel was left alone, without strength, listening to the man's words but not able to respond. All he could do was stand there and stare at this great vision, and then he fell to the earth in a deep sleep.

Who was this man? Was he an angel sent to assure Daniel that God's heavenly armies would care for the Jewish people and see to it God's will was accomplished?[2] Was it Gabriel, who had already visited Daniel? Or was it a preincarnate appearance of Jesus Christ, the Son of God? Students of the Scriptures have ably defended each of these three views, and so it's unlikely we can be dogmatic. If we decide that this glorious man is the same being who touched Daniel and spoke to him (Dan. 10:10–15), then we will have to opt for Gabriel or another angel, because it's not likely that Jesus would need help from Michael to defeat an evil angel (v. 13). However, it appears that the being who touched Daniel and spoke to him is different from the glorious man that appeared in the vision (see NASB and NIV), and most students think it was Gabriel.

The description of the glorious man resembles the description of the glorified Christ given in Revelation 1:12–16—and John's response was the same as Daniel's! Daniel had already seen the Son of Man at the throne of God in heaven (Dan. 7:9–14), but this man was on the earth and very near to Daniel. I believe that this was a vision of the glorious Son of God and that the angel who spoke to Daniel was Gabriel. But why would the Son of God appear to Daniel at this time?

Frequently in the biblical account of salvation history, you find the Lord Jesus Christ appearing to His servants at special times, either to deliver a special message or to prepare them for a special ministry. He usually appeared in a fashion compatible with their circumstances or their calling. To Abraham, the pilgrim, Jesus came as a traveler (Gen. 18), but to Jacob the schemer, He came as a wrestler (Gen. 32). Before Joshua attacked Jericho, Jesus came as Captain of the Lord's armies (Josh. 5:13–15), and to Isaiah, He revealed Himself as the King on the throne (Isa. 6; John 12:37–41). But to the two Jewish exiles—Daniel in Babylon and the apostle John on Patmos—Jesus appeared as the glorified King-Priest. After seeing the Son of God, both men were given visions of future events that involved the people of God, events that would be difficult to accept and understand.

At the beginning of Daniel's prophetic ministry, he interpreted the meaning of the awesome image that King Nebuchadnezzar had seen in his dream (Dan. 2), and now at the end of his ministry, Daniel saw an even greater sight—the glorious King of Kings and Lord of Lords! When we know that Jesus is standing with us and fighting for us, we can accept any circumstance and accomplish any task He gives us.

Apart from the prophetic significance, there is a sense in which Daniel's experience by the Tigris River conveys a lesson to all Christian leaders. There is a price to pay if we're to see what God wants us to see and hear what He is saying to us. Daniel didn't have this great vision early in his ministry but at the end of a long and faithful life. "Blessed are the pure in heart: for they shall see God" (Matt. 5:8). Spiritual leaders often see what others can't see and hear what they fail to hear. They must stand when others flee, and they must receive God's message even if it makes them feel weak and helpless. By seeing the greatness and glory of God, Daniel was prepared to accept and record the prophetic message the angels brought.

The angel had come to give Daniel a special revelation concerning the Jewish people and what would happen to them in the latter days (Dan. 10:14). As we study this complex prophecy, we must focus on Israel and not on the church, even though all Scripture is profitable for all believers at all times. Parts of this prophecy have already been fulfilled, but much of it remains to be fulfilled in "the end times," that is, during the seventieth week of the "prophetic calendar" given in verses 24–27.

AN INVISIBLE WAR (10:10–21)

We get the impression that the glorious man clothed in linen vanished from the scene and one of the angels, perhaps Gabriel, touched Daniel. The old prophet was on his face on the ground, but the ministry of the angel enabled him to lift himself to his hands and knees. Then the angel spoke to him, and this gave him the strength to stand upright. This reminds us that the angels ministered to our Lord after His temptation (Matt. 4:11; Mark 1:13) and in the garden when He prayed (Luke 22:41–43). This is the third time Daniel was touched by an angel (Dan. 8:18; 9:21; and see 10:16, 18–19).

This is the second time Daniel was addressed as "dearly beloved" (9:23; and see 10:19). We recall that our Lord Jesus Christ was spoken of this way by the Father (Matt. 3:17; 17:5; Mark 1:11; 9:7; 12:6; Luke 3:22; 20:13;

and cf. Isa. 42:1–4 with Matt. 12:15–21). Because we His children are "in Christ," we are "accepted in the beloved" (Eph. 1:6), and the Father loves us as He loves His Son (John 17:23, 26). It isn't enough for us to know that God loves us; we must so live in fellowship with Him that we "keep [ourselves] in the love of God" (Jude 21; John 14:19–24).

Daniel's conversation with the angel reveals to us the important fact that there is an "invisible war" going on in the heavenlies between the forces of evil and the forces of God. For three weeks, Daniel had been praying for wisdom to understand the visions he had already seen, but the answer to that prayer was delayed. Why would the Lord not immediately answer the petitions of His beloved prophet? Because "the prince of the kingdom of Persia"—an evil angel—had attacked the angel bearing the answer, probably Gabriel. This evil angel was assigned to see to it that the king of Persia did what Satan wanted him to do. Michael, the archangel assigned to minister to Israel (Dan. 12:1; Rev. 12:7; Jude 9), assisted Gabriel and together they won the battle.

Well-meaning people may scoff at the idea of demonic forces and good and evil angels, and they may caricature Satan, but the fact remains that this is biblical theology. When Lucifer rebelled against God and was judged, some of the angels fell with him and became the demonic evil angels that oppose Christ and obey Satan (Isa. 14:12–15; Rev. 12:7–12; Matt. 25:41). According to Ephesians 6:10–18, Satan has a well-organized army of evil spirits that obey his every command. Through His sacrificial work on the cross, Christ defeated Satan and his army (1:20–23; Col. 2:15; John 12:31; Rev. 12:11), and we can claim that victory by faith. The believer's responsibility is to put on the whole armor of God by faith and use the Word of God and believing prayer to oppose and defeat the wicked one.

It appears that there are specific evil angels assigned to various nations; some students of angelology call them "territorial spirits." That's why Paul told the Ephesian believers that the Christian's battle was not against flesh and blood but against demonic forces in the heavenlies that oppose the holy angels who always do God's will. The problems that the Jewish remnant were having in Jerusalem at that time weren't being caused by the local officials but by Satan's evil powers using those officials. Christians are never to worship angels (Col. 2:18–19; Rev. 19:10; 22:8–9) or pray to angels, for our worship and prayer belong to God alone. But when we pray, God directs the armies of heaven to fight on our behalf, even though we may know nothing about the battles that are being waged in this invisible war. (See 2 Kings 6:17.)

The prophet Daniel realized the great significance of God's plans for Israel, and once again he fainted and was unable to speak. Here he had been involved in a cosmic spiritual conflict and didn't even know it, and the Lord was using some of His highest angels to answer his prayers! This certainly lifts prayer out of the level of a humdrum religious exercise and shows it to be one of our strongest and most important spiritual weapons. The neglect of prayer is the reason why many churches and individual believers are so weak and defeated. The late Peter Deyneka, missionary to the Slavic peoples, often reminded us, "Much prayer, much power; no prayer, no power!" Jesus taught His disciples that the demonic forces could not be defeated except by prayer and fasting, the very activities that Daniel had been involved in for three weeks (Matt. 17:14–21).

Our Lord Jesus took seriously the reality of Satan and his demonic forces, and so should we. This doesn't mean we should blame every headache and interruption on the demons, but it does mean we should respect Satan's power (like a roaring lion, 1 Peter 5:8) and his subtlety (like a serpent, 2 Cor. 11:3). One of Satan's chief traps is to get people to think he doesn't exist or, if he does exist, he's not worth worrying about.

Once again, the angel restored Daniel's strength so he could hear the prophetic message from the messenger and record for our learning. Twice the angels told him, "Fear not" (Dan. 10:12, 19). The angel also said, "Peace! Be strong now; be strong" (v. 19 NIV). Daniel needed strength to be able to hear the long message the angel brought to him.

Finally, the angel made it clear that the battle wasn't yet over. As soon as he finished instructing Daniel, Gabriel would return to assist Michael in battling the prince of Persia and the prince of Greece, two satanic evil angels who were opposing the plans of the Lord for these nations. The ruler of Persia had shown great kindness and mercy to the Jews in allowing them to return home, and Satan was against this decision. God also had plans for Greece (11:2–4) and Satan wanted to interfere there. One reason why God commands His people to pray for those in authority is so that God's will, not Satan's plans, might be fulfilled in their lives (1 Tim. 2:1–3). The destiny of more than one nation has been changed because God's people have fervently prayed.

"For the weapons of our warfare are not carnal but mighty in God for pulling down strongholds, casting down arguments and every high thing that exalts itself against the knowledge of God, bringing every thought into captivity to the obedience of Christ" (2 Cor. 10:4–5 NKJV).

QUESTIONS FOR PERSONAL REFLECTION
OR GROUP DISCUSSION

1. Daniel fasted and prayed to gain understanding. What kinds of things do you do to gain understanding from God?

   To gain more understanding I study, pray and try to be obedient to his Spirit.

2. When you face a circumstance in life in which it seems God's agenda is not being accomplished, how do you decide whether to sit back and let God do His work or to jump in and start making things happen?

   It depends. If there is nothing.

3. Daniel was given a vision of Christ. How do you think this prepared him for a difficult message? *A message from the designer would definitely improve the communication & preparation.*

4. In what ways would seeing Jesus in person make you better able to face life? *Seeing the Master in person would improve faith*

5. How does it make you feel to think that a whole spiritual war is being waged around you between the power of God and the power of evil?

   I know that the powers of evil is penetrated in this evil world.

6. In what ways is prayer a powerful weapon in that war?

   Pray is a powerful weapon because it works

7. How do you discern if a difficult circumstance is just "life happening" or if it is evidence of spiritual warfare? *I am not sure.*

8. What are some other ways, besides prayer, that we add strength to God's army in the spiritual battles of life?
   Be active, study, witnessing, giving

9. What do you consider to be your strongest weapon against Satan's attacks? *Prayer & fasting*

10. What kinds of things make your prayers the most potent that they can be? *believe in faith —*

   A
   C
   T
   S

INTERLUDE

The prophecy given in chapters 11 and 12 is long and complex. The first thirty-five verses of Daniel 11 were prophecy in Daniel's day but are now history. They deal with important but, for the most part, forgotten historical characters with difficult names and complicated relationships. The chapters may be outlined as follows:

1. Prophecies already fulfilled (Daniel 11:1–35)
   a. About Persia (Daniel 11:1–2)
   b. About Greece (Daniel 11:3–4)
   c. About Egypt and Syria (Daniel 11:5–20)
   d. About Antiochus Epiphanes and Syria (Daniel 11:21–35)
2. Prophecies yet to be fulfilled (Daniel 11:36—12:3)
   a. About the tribulation and Antichrist (Daniel 11:36—12:1)
   b. About the promised kingdom (Daniel 12:2–3)
   c. Final instructions to Daniel (Daniel 12:4–13)

These prophecies fill in the details of previous prophecies the Lord had given to Daniel and were the answer to his prayer for greater understanding of God's plans for Israel. The focus is on Israel in the last days.

A REMARKABLE PROPHECY—PART I

(Daniel 11:1–35)

F ulfilled prophecy is one of the proofs of the inspiration of the Bible, for only an omniscient God can know future events accurately and direct His servants to write them down. "He reveals deep and secret things; He knows what is in the darkness, and light dwells with Him" (Dan. 2:22 NKJV). It is no surprise, then, that the radical critics have attacked the book of Daniel, and especially these chapters, because they claim that nobody could write in advance so many accurate details about so many people and events. Their "scientific conclusion" is that the book of Daniel is a fraud; it was written centuries after these events, and therefore is not a book of prophecy at all. These critics can't deny the historicity of the events, because the records are in the annals of ancient history for all to read and cannot be denied. Therefore, to maintain their "scientific theories," they must deny the reality of prophecy.[1] Those of us who believe in a great God have no problem accepting "the word of prophecy" (2 Peter 1:19–21).

First, we will consider the verses that were prophecy in Daniel's day but have been fulfilled and are now ancient history. As we do, we will try to glean some practical spiritual lessons to help us in our Christian walk today.

PROPHECIES ABOUT PERSIA (11:1–2)

It's likely that verse 1 should be at the end of the previous chapter since it deals with the holy angels' conflict with Satan's angels. The rulers of Persia had no idea that Satan was seeking to control their minds and lead them into making decisions that would hurt the people of God. The Persian rulers were much more considerate of the Jews than were the Babylonian rulers, and Satan didn't want this to happen. He hates the Jews and is the father of anti-Semitism wherever it is found (Rev. 12). However, Michael and Gabriel won that battle, and Darius and Cyrus showed compassion for the Jewish exiles. In fact, it was Cyrus who issued the important edict that permitted the Jews to return to their land and rebuild their temple (Ezra 1:1–4).

The four kings that would rule in the future were Cambyses (529–522), Pseudo-Smerdis (522–521), Darius I Hystapes (521–486), and Xerxes (496–465), the Ahasuerus of the book of Esther.

Cambyses was the son and successor of Cyrus the Great, and perhaps is the Ahasuerus of Ezra 4:6. His passionate ambition was to invade Egypt and regain the territory that Nebuchadnezzar had gained but that was later lost. Cambyses manufactured an excuse for the war, saying that he had asked for the hand in marriage of one of the Egyptian princesses but had been rejected by her father. He did conquer Egypt, but when he tried to take Ethiopia and Carthage, he failed miserably and had to retreat. He ruled Egypt with an iron hand and gave every evidence of being insane. He married two of his sisters, murdered his brother and heir Smerdis, and then murdered the sister who protested the murder of the brother. One of the leading Persian priests plotted an insurrection and seized the throne, taking the name of the dead prince. (Historians call him Pseudo-Smerdis.) Cambyses died while marching home to unseat the new king, who reigned for about a year.

But the most important of the four kings, and the wealthiest, was

Xerxes I, the Ahasuerus of the book of Esther. He ruled an empire that reached from Ethiopia to India and he had a great passion to conquer Greece. In 480 he tried to invade Greece, but his vast fleet was defeated at Salamis and Samos, and his army was defeated at Plataea. All of this occurred between chapters 1 and 2 of the book of Esther. He came home a bitter and angry man and sought to find relief for his wounded pride by enjoying his harem. It was at this time that Esther entered the picture. Xerxes was assassinated in August 465.

PROPHECIES ABOUT GREECE (11:3–4)
From the previous visions, Daniel already knew the sequence of the great empires.

The mighty king of 11:3 is, of course, Alexander the Great, who was determined to punish the Persians for Xerxes' invasion. We have already met Alexander and know about his vast army and his lightning-like conquest of the nations. Indeed, he did what he pleased and nobody could stand in his way. In 332, Alexander defeated the Persians and in 323 he died and his kingdom was divided among four of his generals.

Once again, Alexander's incredible conquests were part of the sovereign plan of God. The spread of the Greek language and Greek culture assisted in the eventual spread of the gospel and the Greek New Testament. Alexander's goal was not just to conquer territory but to bring people together in a "united empire." His soldiers married women from the conquered nations, and Alexander's empire became a "melting pot" for all peoples. This too assisted in the spread of the gospel centuries later.

THE KINGS OF THE NORTH AND THE SOUTH (11:5–20)
The nations here are Egypt (south) and Syria (north), and the rulers change regularly. The little nation of Israel was caught between these two great

powers and was affected by their conflicts. All of these people and events may not be interesting to you, but the prophecies Daniel recorded tally with the record of history, thus proving that God's Word can be trusted. The Ptolemy line provided the rulers in Egypt, and the Seleucid line the rulers in the north (Syria). These paragraphs are merely summary statements, but if you read them in the light of the related verses, you will see how Daniel's prophecies were fulfilled. Along with reading your KJV, you may also want to read these verses in the NASB or the NIV.

Ptolemy I Soter and Seleucus I Nicator (v. 5). Seleucus was the stronger of the two and ruled over a large empire, but it was his alliance with Ptolemy that enabled him to seize the throne of Syria.

Ptolemy II Philadelphus and Antiochus II Theos (v. 6). As was often done in the days of monarchies, the rulers used marriage as a means of forming strong political alliances, a policy Solomon had followed (1 Kings 3:1; 11:1ff.). However, Ptolemy demanded that Antiochus divorce his wife Laodice in order to marry his daughter Berenice. Ptolemy died after two years, so Seleucus took back his former wife, who then murdered both him and Berenice. It was one marriage where they all didn't live happily ever after. "She will not retain her power, and he and his power will not last" (Dan. 11:6 NIV).

Ptolemy III Euergetes and Seleucus II Callinicus (vv. 7–9). The new king of Egypt was the brother of Berenice, and he was intent on defending his sister's honor and avenging her death. He attacked the northern power, won the victory, and collected a great deal of wealth. Then the two kings ignored each other for some years until Seleucus attacked Egypt in 240, was defeated, and had to return home in shame. He was killed by a fall from his horse, and his son Seleucus III Soter took the throne, only to be assassinated four years later. Antiochus III the Great, who ruled from 223 to 187, succeeded him.

Ptolemy IV Philopater and Antiochus III the Great (vv. 10–19).[2] The sons of Seleucus II were Seleucus III, who was a successful general but was killed in battle, and Antiochus III the Great, who carried out the Syrian military program with great skill. He regained lost territory from Egypt, but in 217 the Egyptian army defeated the Syrians. This didn't stop Antiochus, for he took his army east and got as far as India.

In 201, Antiochus mustered another large army, joined forces with Philip V of Macedon, and headed for Egypt (vv. 13–16), where he won a great victory against Ptolemy V Epiphanes. Contrary to God's law, but in fulfillment of the prophecies (visions), some of the Jews in Palestine joined with Antiochus, hoping to break free of Egyptian control; but their revolt was crushed (v. 14). Antiochus not only conquered Egypt and Sidon (v. 15), but also "the glorious land" of Palestine (v. 16).

Once again marriage enters the scene. Antiochus offered to negotiate with the Egyptian leaders and to marry his daughter Cleopatra I[3] to Ptolemy V, who was seven years old at the time! He hoped that his daughter would undermine the Egyptian government from within and use her position to help him take over. However, Cleopatra was loyal to her husband, so the marriage stratagem didn't succeed.

Antiochus decided to attack Greece but was defeated at Thermopylae (191) and Magnesia (189). The "prince for his own behalf" (v. 18) was the Roman consul and general Lucius Cornelius Scipio Asiaticus, who led the Roman and Greek forces to victory over Antiochus. At an earlier meeting, Antiochus had insulted the Roman general, but the Romans had the last word. The Syrian leader died in 187, and his successor was his son Seleucus IV Philopator, who oppressed the Jewish people by raising taxes so he could pay tribute to Rome. Shortly after he sent his treasurer Heliodorus to plunder the Jewish temple, Seleucus Philopator suddenly died (probably poisoned), thus fulfilling verse 20. This opened the way for the wicked Antiochus Epiphanes to seize the throne.

As you review the history of the relationship between Egypt and Syria,

164 \ Be Resolute

and the family relationships among the Seleucids, you can't help but realize that human nature hasn't changed over these thousands of years. The ancient world had its share of intrigue, political deception, violence, greed, and war. The lust for power and wealth drove men and women to violate human rights and break divine laws, to go to any length to get what they wanted. They slaughtered thousands of innocent people, plundered the helpless, and even killed their own relatives, just to wear a crown or sit on a throne.

While God is not responsible for the evil that men and women have done in the name of government and religion, He is still the Lord of history and continues to work out His plans for humankind. Studying the evil deeds of past rulers could make us cynical, but we must remember that one day "the earth shall be filled with the knowledge of the glory of the LORD, as the waters cover the sea" (Hab. 2:14).

PROPHECIES ABOUT ANTIOCHUS EPIPHANES AND SYRIA (11:21–35)

We have already met this wicked man (8:9–14) who in his character and activities is a picture of the future Antichrist. He gave himself the name "Epiphanes," which means "glorious one," but Gabriel calls him "a vile [contemptible] person." Antiochus wasn't the heir to the throne, but he obtained it by guile. The true heir was Demetrius Soter, who was very young, so Antiochus claimed to be his lawful protector and seized the throne.

He was very successful in his military endeavors and knew how to combine deceptive strategy with brute force. In his first campaign against Egypt (11:25–28), he won the battle even though he failed to take all of Egypt. He sat down at the bargaining table with the Egyptian leaders, never intending to keep any agreements. In spite of deception on both sides, the Lord was still in control and was watching the calendar. He has His appointed times and He is always on time.

On his return to Syria in 170, Antiochus turned his attention to Israel and the wealth in the temple (v. 28). He plundered and defiled the temple, abolished the daily sacrifices, killed a great many Jews, and left soldiers behind to keep things in control. Two years later (168) he again invaded Egypt, but this time the Romans (v. 30, "ships of Chittim") confronted him and told him to stop. He obeyed grudgingly and took out his anger on the Jews, with the help of Jewish traitors who forsook their own covenant to support him. He promised to reward them generously for their help.

On December 14, 168, Antiochus desecrated the temple by erecting an altar to Zeus and by offering a pig as a sacrifice. Gabriel calls this "the abomination that maketh desolate" (v. 31). The future Antichrist will put his own image in the Jewish temple when he breaks his covenant with the Jews in the middle of the seven-year tribulation period, Daniel's seventieth week (9:27; 11:31; 12:11; Matt. 24:15; Mark 13:14). Antiochus was doing his best not only to exterminate the Jewish people but also to eliminate their religion from the earth. He promised to reward the Jews who followed his orders, and there were those who forsook their holy covenant to obey him. This was a time of testing and refining for the Jewish people, when they had to decide to obey the God of their fathers and possibly be slain, or submit to the pagan Syrian leaders and live as traitors to their faith (Dan. 11:34–35).

According to verses 33–35, there was a small group of faithful Jews who opposed the godlessness of Antiochus and trusted God to enable them to fight back. A Jewish priest named Mattathias, with his five sons, gathered an army and were able to fight back. His son Judas, nicknamed Maccabeus ("the hammerer"), was one of the heroes of this revolt. Many Jews laid down their lives for their city, their temple, and their faith, and finally they won. On December 14, 165, the temple was purified and the altar dedicated. (See 8:9–14, 23–25.) The Jews celebrate this occasion annually as the Feast of Lights (Hanukkah). Their enemy Antiochus Epiphanes died in Persia in 163. He was judged insane, and it was no wonder people called him "Antiochus Epimanes—Antiochus the madman."

Gabriel closes this section about Antiochus by reminding Daniel that what he had related to him had implications for Israel in "the time of the end" (11:35). Although he had spoken about leaders who would appear after the fall of Persia, Daniel could see in those events some of the things that would happen to the Jews in the end times. This was especially true of Antiochus Epiphanes, a clear picture of the future Antichrist. Daniel knew that his people would endure great suffering for their faith, that some would apostasize and join the enemy, and that others would trust the Lord and "do exploits" (v. 32). No matter how difficult the times, God has always had His faithful remnant, and He will keep His covenant with His people to the very end.

Having mentioned "the time of the end," Gabriel will now speak about the future Antichrist and the terrible time of Jacob's trouble (11:36—12:1).

QUESTIONS FOR PERSONAL REFLECTION
OR GROUP DISCUSSION

1. How do you respond to the statement, "Fulfilled prophecy is one of the proofs of the inspiration of the Bible"?

   Only God knows the future

2. What are some current signs that show us that people are still interested in being able to tell the future? *News media,*

3. How often today do you imagine spiritual conflicts are happening in regard to national leaders, as they were in the time of Daniel?

   Quite often

4. Wiersbe points out that God's hand can be seen in Alexander the Great's conquests paving the way for the gospel to spread more easily. In what other places in history have you spotted God's hand at work?

   Roman Roads, Gutenburg Printing press, Columbus discovering the Americans,

5. From the sounds of it, marriage and politics were never far apart in Daniel's day. In your perspective, how does that compare with the political climate today? *I am sure it does. Those who have good marriages make good leaders.*

6. What is the significance to you of the fact that Daniel not only foretold other events in the Bible, but also events recorded in secular history?

Daniel was listening to God who sets up nations

7. How is it that the heart of man can contain so much evil and yet God can fulfill His purposes through him? *God is very creative. He has defeated satan through the cross*

8. Wiersbe describes the time of Antiochus's evil rule as a refining time for God's people. List some other times throughout history that have refined God's people. *Monsters, Great revivals, Crusades, World Wars, & Civil War Global warming*

9. When faced with persecution, what are the factors that make people turn back on their faith? *Facing fear, Needing & Depending on faith, Reading the covenant*

10. When faced with persecution (as the Jews suffered under Antiochus and Christians will suffer under the Antichrist), what are the factors that make people stand firm even to their own death?

*Teamwork
Truth
Trust
Training*

Chapter Twelve

A REMARKABLE PROPHECY—PART II

(Daniel 11:36—12:13)

A t Daniel 11:36, the prophecy shifts from Antiochus Epiphanes to the man he foreshadowed, the Antichrist, the last world dictator.[1] We have moved to "the time of the end" (v. 35; see 12:4), when the following events are predicted to occur:

- The rise of Antichrist (Daniel 11:36–39)
- The tribulation (Daniel 12:1)
- War and invasions (Daniel 11:40–43)
- The battle of Armageddon (Daniel 11:44–45a)
- The return of Christ to defeat Antichrist (Daniel 11:45b)
- The resurrection of the dead (Daniel 12:2)
- The glorious kingdom (Daniel 12:3)[2]

THE TIME OF TRIBULATION (11:36—12:1)

Both the Old Testament and the New Testament teach that a time of great tribulation will one day come to the world, and our interpretation of Daniel's seventy weeks (9:24–27) locates this period in the last "week" of his prophecy. The event that triggers the beginning of those last seven years is the signing of the covenant with Israel by the powerful leader in the ten-nation confederacy in Europe (see 7:7–28). The reason for the covenant seems to be the guarantee of his protection for Israel while the Jews rebuild their temple in Jerusalem. The tribulation period will end with the return of Christ and the confinement of Antichrist and Satan in the lake of fire (Rev. 19:11–21).

The rise of Antichrist (vv. 36–39). This evil ruler doesn't suddenly appear in his true character and assume leadership over the world. He begins his rise to power as a part of the ten-nation European coalition; he is the "little horn" that emerges from the ten horns (7:24ff.). He begins as a man of peace who "solves" the Arab/Israeli problem and proves himself to be a master politician.[3] Gradually his evil designs are revealed, and at the middle of the seven-year period, he will break that covenant, claim world control, and set himself up as god (9:27; 2 Thess. 2; Rev. 13).

Gabriel describes this evil ruler (king) as a selfish and willful person, a spellbinding orator who will arrogantly exalt himself. He is a man with no religious faith. He shall have a successful career until the tribulation ends with the return of Jesus Christ to set up His kingdom.[4] "He [Antichrist] shall come to his end, and none shall help him" (Dan. 11:45). Since verse 37 uses the phrase "the God of his fathers," does this mean that this world ruler must be Jewish? Some hold that the answer is yes, arguing that the nation of Israel would not sign a pact with a Gentile, but no Scripture supports such a view. Over the centuries, the Jews have often negotiated with political leaders who were not Jewish. The phrase "God of our fathers" (or "Lord God of our fathers") does indeed refer to the God of Israel (Deut. 26:7; 1 Chron. 12:17; 2 Chron. 20:6; Ezra 7:27; Acts 3:13; 5:30; 22:14), but that may not be the meaning in Daniel 11:37. The phrase can be translated "the gods of his fathers" as is done by both the NIV and the NASB.[5] The Antichrist will be an atheist and reject all religions except the one he establishes when he declares himself "god."

Some have suggested that his rejection of "the desire of women" indicates that he has a homosexual orientation. But the phrase "desire of women" probably relates to Haggai 2:7, a title of the Messiah, for it was the desire of Jewish women to give birth to the promised Messiah. Not only will Antichrist reject all religion in general but he will oppose the Jewish religion in particular, especially the hope their Messiah will return and deliver them from their enemies. His god is the god of might and of military power. When the people of the world worship the man of sin, they are actually worshipping Satan, the one who empowers the Antichrist. Like Antiochus centuries before him, Antichrist will reward those who worship him and his manufactured god.

The tribulation (12:1). "At that time" means "during the time of the end," the time period the angel is describing in this part of the prophecy. We have now reached the middle of the tribulation when Antichrist breaks his covenant with Israel, seizes the temple, and sets himself up as world dictator and god. This is the "abomination of desolation" that Daniel wrote about in 9:27; 11:31; and 12:11, and that Jesus referred to in His Olivet Discourse (Matt. 24:15; Mark 13:14). The last three and a half years of Daniel's seventieth week will usher in a time of terrible suffering. "For then shall be great tribulation, such as was not since the beginning of the world to this time, no, nor ever shall be," said Jesus (Matt. 24:21; and see Rev. 13—19).

One of the features of this terrible time will be Antichrist's (Satan's) war against the Jewish people (Rev. 12), but Michael, the angel assigned to care for the Jewish people (Dan. 10:13, 21; Rev. 12:7), will come to their aid. God's elect people will be preserved (Matt. 24:22). This will include the 144,000 who are sealed by the Lord (Rev. 7:1–8). God will keep His covenant with Abraham and see to it that the Jewish remnant will enter into their promised kingdom.

Military invasion (11:40–43). When Antichrist moves into the land of Israel and sets up his image in the Jewish temple and declares himself the ruler and god of the whole world, not everybody will bow down to his will. The kings of the north and the south will oppose him and bring their armies to Palestine. In previous prophecies in Daniel, the king of the south has been Egypt and the king of the north has been Syria, but those designations may not apply to the nations in the end times. Some students equate this invasion with the battle described in Ezekiel 38—39, and they see in it a northern confederacy headed by Russia and a southern confederacy headed by Egypt and its allies.[6] The Antichrist will overcome his enemies and acquire great wealth as a result.

Armageddon (11:44–45). Throughout the last three and a half years of the tribulation period, nations will submit to the rule of Antichrist, but there will be growing dissent and opposition, even though his work is energized by Satan. The news report in verse 44 refers to the growing army from the east that will meet the forces of Antichrist on the Plain of Esdraelon to fight what is called "the battle of Armageddon" (Rev. 9:13–21; 16:12–16; Joel 3:1–2, 12–14; Zech. 14:1–3). The word *Armageddon* means "mountain of Megiddo," and this battle ("campaign") occurs at the end of the tribulation period.

The return of Christ. As the huge army from the east gets positioned to attack the forces of Antichrist in Israel, the sign of the returning Son of Man will appear in the heavens (Matt. 24:29–30), and the opposing armies will unite to fight Jesus Christ. But the Lord will descend from heaven with His armies, defeat both armies, and take captive Satan, Antichrist, and the false prophet and cast them into the lake of fire (Rev. 19:11–21; see also Zech. 12:1–9; 14:1–3). "He [Antichrist] shall come to his end, and no one shall help him" (Dan. 11:45).

Daniel doesn't reveal this truth, but the prophet Zechariah promises that the nation of Israel will see their Messiah as He comes from heaven, recognize Him, repent of their sins, and trust Him, and the nation will be cleansed (Zech. 12:10—13:1). Jesus will stand on the Mount of Olives (14:4; Acts 1:11–12), "and the LORD shall be king over all the earth" (Zech. 14:9) and will establish His glorious kingdom for a thousand years (Rev. 20:1–7).

THE KINGDOM (12:2–3)

Six times in Revelation 20:1–7 you find the words "thousand years." The Latin for "thousand years" (*mille, annum*) gives us the English word *millennium*, the word we use for the time when Christ will reign on earth. Those Christians who believe that the Old Testament prophecies of a kingdom on earth will be fulfilled literally are called "millennialists"; those who reject this view are called "amillennialists"—not millennialists. They usually spiritualize the Old Testament prophecies of the Jewish kingdom and apply them to the church today. Certainly there are spiritual applications to the church from the Old Testament kingdom prophecies, but the basic interpretation seems to be that there will be a literal kingdom on earth with Jesus Christ as King and His people reigning with Him. (See Isa. 2:1–5; 4:1–6; 11:1–9; 12:1–6; 30:18–26; 35:1–10.)

The Father has promised a kingdom to His Son (Ps. 2; Luke 1:30–33), and He will keep His promise. One day Jesus will deliver that promised kingdom up to the Father (1 Cor. 15:24). Knowing the Father's promise, Satan tempted Jesus by offering Him all the kingdoms of the world in return for His worship (Matt. 4:8–10); and Jesus refused. Jesus affirmed the kingdom promise to His disciples (Luke 22:29–30), and when they asked Him when it would be fulfilled (Acts 1:6–8), He only told them not to speculate about the times but to get busy doing the work He left them to do. However, He didn't deny the fact that one day there would be a kingdom. Paul used the return of Christ and the establishment of the future kingdom to motivate Timothy in his ministry (2 Tim. 4:1ff.), and this promise ought to be a motivating factor in our lives.

Resurrection (v. 2). The doctrine of the resurrection of the human body is hinted at in the Old Testament but isn't presented with the clarity found in the New Testament. When Abraham went to Mount Moriah to offer up Isaac, he believed that God could raise his son from the dead (Gen. 22; Heb. 11:19). Job expected to see God in his resurrection body (Job 19:25–27), and this anticipation was shared by the writers of the psalms (17:15; 49:15; 71:20). The prophets believed in a future resurrection (Isa. 25:7; Hos. 13:14). Jesus brought "life and immortality to light" (2 Tim. 1:10) and clearly taught the fact of His own resurrection as well as what the resurrection meant to His followers (John 5:19–30; 11:17–44). First Corinthians 15 is the great resurrection chapter in the Bible.

Resurrection is not "reconstruction"; the Lord doesn't put back together the body that has turned to dust (Gen. 3:19), for that dust has become a part of other bodies as people eat food grown in the soil. The resurrection body is a new and glorious body. The relationship between the body that's buried and the body that's raised is like that of a seed to the mature plant (1 Cor. 15:35–53). There is continuity (the plant comes from the seed) but not identity (the plant is not identical to the seed). The burial of a body is like the planting of a seed, and the resurrection is the harvest.

When Jesus Christ returns in the air to call His church, the dead in Christ will be raised first, and then the living believers will be caught up with them to be with the Lord (1 Thess. 4:13–18). When Jesus returns to earth at the end of the tribulation, He will bring His people with Him to share in the victory and the glory. At that time, the Old Testament saints and the tribulation martyrs will be raised to enter into the kingdom. However, those who died without faith in Christ will not be raised until after the Kingdom

Age, and they will be judged (Rev. 20:4–6, 11–15). As Daniel states it, some will awake to enjoy the glorious life with God, and some will awake (a thousand years later) to enter into shame and everlasting contempt—and everlasting judgment.[7] Hell is called "the second death" (Rev. 20:14). If you have been born only once, you can die twice; but if you have been born twice—born again through faith in Christ—you can die only once.

Reward (v. 3). How we have lived and served will determine the rewards the Lord will give us at the judgment seat of Christ (Rom. 14:9–12; 2 Cor. 5:6–10). Every cup will be full in heaven, but some cups will be larger than others. We will share in the glory of Christ, and those who have sought to win others to Christ will shine like the stars in the heavens. There is a special application here to those who have faithfully witnessed during the tribulation period, when it will be a costly thing to identify with Christ and His people (Matt. 24:14; Rev. 7:9–17).

Our Lord emphasized the truth that faithfulness to Him today will lead to reward and ministry in the future kingdom (Matt. 13:43; 19:27–28; 25:14–30; Luke 19:12–27; Rev. 2:26–27; 5:9–10). During His reign on earth, we will share in whatever work He has for us to do, according to how we have lived for Him and served Him here on earth. Believers who have suffered in their service for Christ will be more than compensated as they share in His glory (Rom. 8:18; 2 Cor. 4:7–18).

FINAL INSTRUCTIONS TO DANIEL (12:4–13)

The servant of the Lord never has to fret over what to do next, for the Lord always has a word of encouragement and instruction for him at the right time. During all of his long life, Daniel prayed faithfully, studied the Scriptures, and sought to serve God, and the Lord always guided him, protected him, and used him for His glory. We today are able to study prophecy because Daniel was faithful in his day.

The book (v. 4). In the ancient world, official transactions were ratified with two documents, one that was sealed and kept in a safe place and one that was kept available (Jer. 32:1–12). God looked upon Daniel's book as the "deed" that guaranteed that He would faithfully keep His promises to the people of Israel. To close up the book and seal it didn't mean to hide it away, because God's message was given so His people would know the future. The book was to be treasured and protected and shared with the Jewish people. However, the book was "sealed" in this sense: The full meaning of what Daniel wrote would not be understood until "the time of the end" (see Matt. 24:15). Even Daniel didn't fully understand all that he saw, heard, and wrote (Dan. 12:8)!

When the apostle John completed the book of Revelation, he was told to keep the book unsealed because the time was at hand (Rev. 22:10). We need the book of Daniel so we can better understand the book of Revelation. At least seventy-one passages from Daniel are quoted or alluded to in sixteen New Testament books, most of them in the book of Revelation. All of Daniel 6 is referred to in Hebrews 11:33.

"Many shall run to and fro, and knowledge shall be increased" is not a reference to automobiles and jet planes or the advancement of education. It has reference to the study of God's Word in the last days, especially the study of prophecy. Amos 8:11–12 warns us that the day will come when there will be a famine of God's Word, and people will run here and there seeking for truth but won't find it. But God's promise to Daniel is that, in the last days, His people can increase in their knowledge of prophetic Scripture as they apply themselves to the Word of God. Some interpret "to and fro" to mean running one's eyes to and fro over the pages of Scripture.

The times (vv. 5–7). Two more angels arrived on the scene, one on each side of the Tigris River. The man clothed in linen refers to the awesome person Daniel saw at the beginning (10:5–6), probably Jesus Christ. When one of the angels asked, "How long shall it be to the end of these wonders?" the Lord replied, "for a time, times, and [a] half," that is, three and a half years (12:6–7). The last half of the tribulation period is described in several ways: time, times, and half a time (12:7 NKJV; Rev. 12:14); forty-two months (Rev. 11:2; 13:5); and 1,260 days (11:3). Once the treaty is signed between Antichrist and Israel, the clock starts ticking off seven years, and once Antichrist sets himself up as god in the temple, the last half of Daniel's seventieth week begins. The Lord Jesus spoke this under oath, raising both hands to heaven, so it is certain.

The key to God's timing is the purpose He fulfills for "the holy people," the nation of Israel. Throughout the book of Daniel, the emphasis is on the nation of Israel, and the only reason other nations are mentioned is because of their relationship to the Jews. While the tribulation period is a time for punishing the Gentile nations for the way they have sinned against the Jews (Joel 3:2–8), it's also a time for sifting and purging Israel and preparing the Jews for the return of their Messiah (Amos 9:9–12).

The end (vv. 8–13). "How long?" and "How will it end?" are questions that we ask when the times are difficult and the future in doubt. "What's the purpose of it all?" Daniel did what all of us must do: he humbly asked God for the wisdom that he needed. But He may not tell us (Deut. 29:29)! He knows how much we need to know and how much we can take (John 16:12). He did promise that all these things would be clearer for those living in the end times, which is an encouragement for us to prayerfully study the prophetic Scriptures.

But the Lord did reveal that, in the end times, as trials come to the people on the earth, these trials will make the believers purer and wiser, but the wicked will only become more wicked. "But evil men and impostors will grow worse and worse, deceiving and being deceived" (2 Tim. 3:13 NKJV; see Rev. 22:11). The unbelievers will be ignorant of the truth but the believers will have their eyes opened to the truths of the Word. The word of prophecy is our light when things get dark (2 Peter 1:19).

The significance of the 1,290 days and the 1,335 days isn't made clear, but there is a blessing attached to the second number. The starting point is the middle of the tribulation, when the abomination of desolation is set up in the temple. Since there are 1,260 days (three and a half years) before the tribulation ends, the 1,290 days would take us 30 days beyond the return of the Lord, and the 1,335 days 75 days beyond the end of the tribulation. We aren't told why these days are important or how they will be used to bring blessing to God's people. Certainly there are activities that the Lord must direct and tasks to accomplish, all of which will take time. Perhaps the greatest task is the regathering of His people from the nations of the world (Ezek. 20:33–38; Isa. 1:24—2:5; 4:2–6; 11:1–16), their purging, and their preparation to enter the promised kingdom.

Though the Lord had taught Daniel many things and revealed to him many mysteries, it was not for him to know everything before he died. As the end of his life drew near, it was enough to know that he had been faithful to the Lord and would one day rest from his labors (Rev. 14:13). He will one day be raised from the dead and receive the reward the Lord has allotted for him (Matt. 25:21). "I shall be satisfied, when I awake, with thy likeness" (Ps. 17:15; 1 John 3:1–3; Rom. 8:29).

QUESTIONS FOR PERSONAL REFLECTION
OR GROUP DISCUSSION

1. How often you think about the end times? Why do you think that is?

   I think about the end times when I hear about disasters in the weather, political evils, + evil in the news. Globe warming

2. What technological and media developments in our current society do you think will pave the way for the Antichrist's rise to power?

   I believe the modern communications advancement, transportation + electronic surveillance could help an evil one.

3. From all that you've heard about the tribulation throughout your life, what seems the most fearful to you? *I have been taught there would be a rapture of the church before the tribulation. Either way God will protect his own.*

4. What is the significance to you that so many people throughout the ages have tried to destroy or hurt the Jewish nation and yet it survives and returns home every time? *The Jewish people have the substance of the Word*

5. What questions do you still wonder about in regard to the rapture?

   In the rapture - is our Lord coming or going

6. How do you think the typical person's lifestyle would be affected if the judgment seat of Christ was brought to his or her mind every day?

   The boss is watching - do your best

7. What parts of Scripture do we need to study besides prophecy to be truly prepared for the Lord's return? *All of it.*

Matt., epistles, Rom., Heb., 1st Thess.

8. Why do you think God revealed information about the end of the world as we know it in such a mysterious and prophetic way?

It is a mystery. God wants us to antipate his coming.

9. How would you describe the balance between prophetic intrigue, *christy* personal devotion, and fervent evangelism in terms of our responsibility to God? *We should be ready, desiring to know God's future for our lives & shear our faith w the world*

10. What is the role of the knowledge we gain from the prophecies of Daniel in regard to our everyday lives before God?

Chapter Thirteen

A RESOLUTE MAN GOD GREATLY LOVED

(A Review of Daniel)

I t's important to study the prophecies that Daniel wrote, but it's also important to understand the life that Daniel lived. Knowing God's future plan and obeying God's present will should go together. "And everyone who has this hope in Him purifies himself, just as He is pure" (1 John 3:3 NKJV). "Therefore, since all these things will be dissolved, what manner of persons ought you to be in holy conduct and godliness?" (2 Peter 3:11 NKJV)

Both Daniel and Joseph were called of God to serve Him in difficult places at the center of authority in pagan empires. Both were cruelly taken from their homes and handed over to foreign masters. Both went through periods of testing, both were lied about and falsely accused, but both maintained godly character and conduct and became respected leaders in the nation. Most of all, both were able to minister to God's people and help preserve and encourage the nation of Israel when the days were difficult. What Daniel wrote gave the Jews courage in the centuries following their release from captivity, and it will encourage them in the end times when they again experience severe persecution from their enemies.

It's interesting to note that the book of Daniel and Paul's letter to the Ephesians have much in common. Ephesians teaches us about the spiritual battle in the heavenlies (Eph. 6:10–18), and Daniel participated in such a battle (Dan. 10:10–21). Paul prays two prayers in Ephesians, the first for enlightenment (Eph. 1:15–23) and the second for enablement (3:14–21). Daniel and his friends also prayed that way, that they might understand God's plan and receive the power they needed to serve Him and remain true to the end.

Paul's epistle to the Ephesians emphasizes the spiritual posture of believers: We are seated with Christ (2:5–6), we walk with Him (4:1, 17; 5:1–2, 8, 15), we take our stand in Christ (6:11, 13–14), and we bow our knees to Christ (3:14). Daniel was a man who bowed his knees to the Lord, walked with Him, and was able to take his stand against Satan. He was given a place of authority in Babylon, but that was nothing compared to the authority God gave him from the throne of heaven. Daniel was a pilgrim and stranger in Babylon because his home was in Israel, and we are pilgrims and strangers on this earth because our citizenship is in heaven (Phil. 3:20–21). Like Daniel and Joseph, we live in an alien culture with people whose thinking, values, actions, and goals are totally different from and opposed to those of God's people. And yet, just as Daniel and Joseph kept themselves pure and helped to transform people and circumstances, so we can become transformers in our world today.

The key to Daniel's successful life and ministry is given in Daniel 1:8— "But Daniel purposed in his heart that he would not defile himself." He was a resolute man. He wasn't intimidated by powerful people or frightened by difficult circumstances. Like Martin Luther at the Diet of Worms, he said, "Here I stand. I can do no other. God help me. Amen."

But what was the source of this man's courageous and resolute heart? For the answer to that important question, let's review the life of Daniel.

He Believed in a Sovereign God

"The Most High rules in the kingdom of men" (Dan. 4:25, 32 NKJV; 5:21) is one of the basic truths taught in the book of Daniel. Dictators and petty politicians may have thought they were in control, but Daniel knew better. As a devoted Jew, Daniel knew that there was but one true God, the Lord Jehovah, and that He ruled all things with wisdom and power. The Babylonians changed Daniel's address, his name, and his education, and they tried to change his standards, but they couldn't change his theology! God was sovereign when He permitted Babylon to conquer Judah, and He was sovereign in sending Daniel and his friends to Babylon. In every aspect of Daniel's life and service, he depended totally on the God of heaven who is sovereign over all things.

Some people associate sovereignty with slavery, when actually our surrender to God's sovereign will is the first step toward freedom. "And I will walk at liberty, for I seek Your precepts" (Ps. 119:45 NKJV). We can yield ourselves to Him with great confidence because He is our Father, and He loves us too much to harm us and He is too wise to make a mistake.

Nor should divine sovereignty be confused with fatalism, "What will be will be." Fatalism is belief in an impersonal force that's working out its blind but inevitable purposes in this world, whether it's the economic forces of materialism and Communism or the "survival of the fittest" in Darwinian evolution. One is tempted to ask, "What established this force? What keeps it going? If it's inevitable, why can we resist it or choose not to accept it?" The Christian believer's faith is in a personal God, a loving God who plans for us the very best (Jer. 29:11). "The LORD is my shepherd; I shall not want" (Ps. 23:1).

He Had a Disciplined Prayer Life

Jewish people were accustomed to praying at nine o'clock in the morning, noon, and three o'clock in the afternoon, the third, sixth, and ninth hours of the day, and Daniel carried that discipline with him to Babylon. Those who set aside special times of prayer are more likely to "pray without ceasing" (1 Thess. 5:17), for the special times of prayer help to sanctify all times and keep us in touch with God.

When Daniel and his friends needed to know Nebuchadnezzar's dream and understand it, they gave themselves to prayer, and when the Lord gave them the answer, they prayed further and thanked Him (Dan. 2:14–23). When Daniel's life was in danger, he went to his home and prayed, and the Lord delivered him from the lions (6:10). Frequently Daniel asked the Lord or His messengers for wisdom to understand the visions the Lord gave to him. Daniel depended on prayer.

In the church today, it seems that many people turn to prayer only when everything else has failed. Their translation of Psalm 46:1 is, "God is our last refuge when our own strength is gone and we don't have anywhere else to turn." What a tragedy! A. W. Tozer used to say, "Whatever God can do, faith can do, and whatever faith can do prayer can do, when it is offered in faith."[1] Daniel not only prayed alone but he also prayed with his friends, because he knew the value of two or three believers assembling together to cry out to God. "I'd rather be able to pray than to be a great preacher," said evangelist D. L. Moody. "Jesus Christ never taught His disciples how to preach, but only how to pray."

HE STUDIED THE WORD OF GOD AND BELIEVED IT

When Daniel and his friends left Jerusalem for Babylon, they carried with them some of the scrolls of the Old Testament Scriptures. We know that Daniel studied the prophecies of Jeremiah (Dan. 9:2), and we can assume that these godly young men had other portions of the Word as well.

Prayer and the Word of God go together (Acts 6:4). Someone asked an old saint, "Which is more important in my Christian life, praying or studying God's Word?" The saint replied, "Which wing on a bird is more important for his flight, the right one or the left one?" As we read the Word of God and study it, we must pray for wisdom to understand and power to obey. We should also turn the Word into prayer. As we pray, we must remember what we've learned from the Scriptures, for the Word increases our faith (Rom. 10:17) and helps us pray in God's will (John 15:7).

Daniel didn't study the Word to impress people; he studied it to ascertain the will of God and obey it. When God enlightened him concerning the seventy years of captivity, Daniel immediately began to pray that God would forgive His people and fulfill His promises, and He did. When you know the Word of God and walk in communion with the God of the Word, you will have a resolute heart and be able to withstand the attacks of the Devil.

He Had an Understanding of Spiritual Warfare

Daniel 10 is a key chapter for prayer warriors, people who wrestle in prayer (Col. 4:12) and seek unto God to tear down the strongholds that block God's truth from getting into the minds of unbelievers (2 Cor. 10:1–6). When I was pastoring the Moody Church in Chicago, I met regularly with three ministerial friends, and together we devoted ourselves to warfare praying. By faith, we sought to attack Satan's strongholds and open the way for the Word of God to change the lives of people in trouble. God gave us many wonderful victories in ways that we could never have imagined.

When by faith we put on the whole armor of God and depend on God's power, God gives us the ability to "stand" and to "withstand" (Eph. 6:10–14). We aren't just brave targets—we're energized combatants! We hold the ground God has given us and we move ahead to capture new ground.

I recognize the fact that the whole concept of spiritual warfare has been abused by some and ridiculed by others, but that shouldn't stop us from imitating great saints like Daniel and Paul who invaded Satan's territory and stood their ground when they were threatened. Isaac Watts said it perfectly:

Are there no foes for me to face?
Must I not stem the flood?
Is this vile world a friend to grace,
    to help me on to God?
Sure I must fight, if I would reign;
    increase my courage, Lord;
I'll bear the toil, endure the pain,
    supported by Thy word.

HE SOUGHT ONLY TO GLORIFY GOD

"There is a God in heaven who reveals secrets," Daniel told the powerful monarch, giving all the glory to the Lord (Dan. 2:28 NKJV), and later Nebuchadnezzar himself was glorifying God (v. 47; 4:34–35). When the king rewarded Daniel for his service, Daniel asked him to include his three friends, for they were an important part of the praying that brought the answer. When Belshazzar tried to smother Daniel with compliments and influence him with gifts, the prophet brushed it all aside and courageously interpreted the bad news to the king (5:13–17).

Throughout his long life, Daniel was a great man in the kingdom, but he used his gifts, abilities, and opportunities to honor God and minister to others. It has well been said that true humility isn't thinking meanly of yourself, it's just not thinking of yourself at all! Jesus came as a servant (Phil. 2), and His example is the one we should follow. I see many leadership conferences for Christians advertised these days; perhaps we need to organize some "servanthood" conferences; for a true leader is always a humble servant. This was true of Joseph, Moses, Joshua, David, and Nehemiah, as well as our Lord and His apostles. Can we improve on what they teach us?

He Realized That He Had a Work to Do

Like Joseph in Egypt, Daniel didn't complain about his lot in life but tried with God's help to make the best use of it. He knew that the sovereign Lord whom he trusted had a special plan for his life and he sought to fulfill it. He didn't campaign for promotions; the Lord brought them to him. He did his work well, he was a faithful and dependable servant, and even his enemies couldn't find anything to criticize (Dan. 6:1–5). If anybody deserved the divine approval of Jesus found in Matthew 25:21, it was Daniel.

Daniel was both a government employee and a prophet of the Lord. God gave him his high position so he could use it to serve the Lord and the Lord's people. The record doesn't tell us, but there may have been many times when Daniel represented the Jewish captives before the king and helped to make life easier for them. He may have influenced the decision of Cyrus to allow the Jews to go back home. We need dedicated believers in places of authority, men and women who can be examples of godliness and instruments of righteousness.

He Was Tactful and Considerate

Some people have the idea that the only way to change things in the political world is to blow up buildings, block traffic, or attack people they consider evil. Daniel exerted considerable influence during the reigns of four kings, and yet he never resorted to force, accusations, or threats. "And a servant of the Lord must not quarrel but be gentle to all" (2 Tim. 2:24 NKJV).

When Daniel and his friends wanted to eat clean food, not food dedicated to idols, they didn't stage a hunger strike or argue with those in charge. Daniel knew that any problems they created would reflect on the prince who was assigned to them and get him into trouble, so he took a different approach. He tactfully asked if they could be tested for ten days, knowing that the Lord would make the test successful. He won the respect and confidence of the prince in charge, and the word got out in the palace that the four Jewish boys in the training classes weren't troublemakers.

Certainly Daniel didn't agree with the theology or lifestyle of the people in charge, but even if he couldn't respect the officers, he respected their offices. (See Paul's teaching on this subject in Rom. 13.) He spoke respectfully to them and about them and cultivated "sound speech that cannot be condemned" (Titus 2:8 NKJV). Too often believers adopt a "holier than thou" attitude and fail to show proper respect for officials they disagree with, and this always hurts the cause of Christ.

He Had Insight into Human History

Scholars have attempted to put together the pieces of the jigsaw puzzle that we call "history," but their best attempts have failed. Like the telephone book, the book of history has a huge cast of characters but no plot. Apart from knowledge of Scripture, we can't interpret history accurately.

At the center of history is the nation of Israel. Why? Because Israel is God's chosen vehicle to bring salvation to the world, for "salvation is of the Jews" (John 4:22). At the center of the Israel's history is God's covenant with Abraham (Gen. 12:1–3) as well as God's covenant with the Jews at Sinai (Ex. 20—24) and in the plains of Moab (Deut. 27—30). If Israel obeyed,

God would bless them and make them a blessing to the Gentiles; if Israel disobeyed, God would discipline and use the Gentile nations to do it.

But the visions also taught Daniel that the nations of the world were beastly in character, like lions, bears, leopards, rams, and goats. Nebuchadnezzar's pride changed him into an animal (Dan. 4), and it is pride that turns leaders into worse than animals as they devour one another. In one sense, our world is improving, and we're grateful for every advancement in medicine, communications, transportation, security, and comfort. But in another sense, the nations of the world are becoming "cheaper and cheaper," as God revealed in the vision of the great image (Dan. 2). It goes from gold to silver, from silver to bronze, from bronze to iron, and from iron to clay! There's not only a decrease in value, but there's also a decrease in strength. By the time you get to the feet and toes of the image, there's nothing but clay to hold it together!

Daniel had no illusions about the future. He knew what the human heart was like and he knew what God had planned to do. No wonder his heart was resolute and nothing moved him or changed him! He could say as Paul did in the storm, "Therefore take heart, men, for I believe God that it will be just as it was told me" (Acts 27:25 NKJV).

He Lived Up to His Name

Daniel means "God is my judge." Daniel lived his life before the all-seeing eyes of the Lord and did the things that pleased Him. He didn't worry about what the king thought of him or his interpretations; he simply delivered the message God gave him and left the results with the Lord. What difference did it make that the other counselors despised him and tried to have him killed? His life and reputation were in the hands of the Lord, and the will of the Lord was always best. Is it any wonder that the Lord greatly loved Daniel?

D. L. Moody often preached on Daniel, and here's an excerpt from one of his messages:

> Daniel thought more of his principles than he did of earthly honor or the esteem of men. Right was right with him. He was going to do right today and let the morrows take care of themselves. That firmness of purpose, in the strength of God, was the secret of his success.[2]

One of Mr. Moody's associates, musician Philip P. Bliss, expressed this truth in a song ("Dare to Be a Daniel") that's not used much today, but the message is certainly needed. The chorus says:

> Dare to be a Daniel,
> Dare to stand alone!
> Dare to have a purpose firm!
> Dare to make it known.

> Be resolute!

QUESTIONS FOR PERSONAL REFLECTION
OR GROUP DISCUSSION

1. What reminders do you have in your life that we are actually aliens in our world much as Daniel was an alien in Babylon?

My life style is different

2. How did Daniel's determination to do what was right enable God to use him?

Daniel's determination brought a difference to his behavior. This brought attention to the King

3. Part of what helped Daniel stay on the right track is that he realized that no matter what happened around him, God was ultimately in control. What distracts us from remembering and gaining strength from that truth?

We get off track by living in our own strength, seeking our own ends, following our own star.

4. How would you describe the strength that a consistent prayer life gives a person?

We gain strength accepting we have the utmost power at our bidding. What we see is not all there is.

5. Daniel studied God's Word to determine how he should live. List some other reasons why people study God's Word.

Studying the word tells us about God. He is omniscient, omnipotent, omnipresent, loving, forgiving, helping us in temptation, and more

6. How do we approach our spiritual journey differently when we are aware of the spiritual warfare going on around us? *Being aware of our spiritual warfare around reminds us we need to fight the good fight of faith, putting on the whole armor of God*

7. Why do you think Daniel remained humble even though he was a national leader? *Daniel remained humble because he was a foreign, believes in Jehovah, sought to do his best in his position of Auth*

8. In what ways do you think we can all have the sense of mission that Daniel did? *We have the same mission that Daniel did because our Lord's command to go into the World & win souls*

9. Daniel and his friends practiced the art of confronting authority while remaining respectful. What sometimes stands in the way of our doing that today? *Some people are political, or national*

10. How can Daniel's story help us live a resolute life?
*Trust God to solve difficult problems
Remain faithful to personal & scriptural convictions
Worship God only*

NOTES

CHAPTER ONE

1. Catherine Drinker Bowen, Miracle at Philadelphia (Boston: Little, Brown and Co., 1966), 125–27.

2. That Daniel wrote the book that bears his name is assumed from 8:1; 9:2, 20; 10:2. That he was an actual historical person is stated not only by his book but also by Ezekiel 14:14, 20; and 28:3, as well as by our Lord in Matthew 24:15 and Mark 13:14.

3. The Babylonians considered the first year of their king's reign "the year of accession" and the next full year his first year, while the Jews began to reckon from the time the king began to reign. That's why Jeremiah 25:1 calls this important year "the fourth year of Jehoiakim," for Jeremiah used Jewish reckoning.

4. This fact shouldn't discourage the rest of us who may not have such special gifts. God prepares and uses all kinds of people, but in the case of the four Hebrew men, excellence was a requirement they had to meet. Use the gifts God has given you and don't compare yourself with others. Each of us is unique.

5. Isaiah had promised that "the king's descendants" would become eunuchs in Babylon (Isa. 39:7).

6. The fact that God used a vegetarian diet to make these four young men succeed doesn't mean that we will succeed if we follow this example. The Bible makes it clear that all foods are permissible to believers (Col. 2:16; Rom. 14:17; Mark 7:1–23; 1 Tim. 4:1–5). The story encourages us to follow their faith, not their diet.

7. Tertullian, "On Prescription Against Heretics" in Alexander Roberts and James Donaldson, *The Ante-Nicene Fathers* (Grand Rapids: Eerdmans, 1976), vol. 3, 246.

8. Op. cit., 51.

9. Andrew Bonar, *Memoir and Remains of Robert Murray M'Cheyne* (London: Banner of Truth Trust, 1966), 29.

Chapter Two

1. From 2:4 to 7:28, the book is written in Aramaic, the language of Babylon, rather than in Hebrew. These prophecies deal primarily with the future of Gentile kingdoms, so Aramaic is more suitable. No doubt Daniel's writings were circulated among the Gentiles as well as the Jews.

2. This name for God is used six times in the book of Daniel—2:18–19, 28, 37, 44; 5:23. It is first heard in Scripture from the lips of Abraham (Gen. 24:3, 7) and is found frequently in Ezra and Nehemiah. It appears to be the name of God used by His people during the years of their exile and dispersion. The God of heaven isn't limited to the land of Israel; He can work even in mighty Babylon!

3. Because Lot was in their city, the people of Zoar escaped the judgment that destroyed the cities of the plain (Gen. 19:18–25), and because Paul was on the ship, God saved all the passengers from drowning

(Acts 27:21–26, 30–32, 42–44). The world opposes God's people, little realizing the blessings that come because of them.

4. A. W. Tozer, *The Set of the Sail* (Camp Hill, PA: Christian Publications, 1986), 33.

5. The "times of the Gentiles" must not be confused with the "fullness of the Gentiles" (Rom. 11:25), when God has gathered into His church all who shall be saved during this present age. This period began at Pentecost and will climax at the rapture of the church. During this time, God is calling out from the Gentiles a people for His name (Acts 15:14). The church is composed of believing Jews and Gentiles, but it is predominantly a Gentile church.

6. Note the use of the pronoun "we" in verse 36. Daniel includes his three friends in the interpreting of the dream.

CHAPTER THREE

1. The furnace is a metaphor for Israel's suffering in Egypt (Deut. 4:20; 1 Kings 8:51; Jer. 11:4); eternal judgment in hell (Matt. 13:42, 50; Rev. 9:2); the holy judgment of the Lord (Gen. 19:28; Ps. 21:9; Isa. 31:9; Mal. 4:1; Rev. 1:15); and times of testing for God's people (Job 23:10; Ps. 66:10; Prov. 17:3; Isa. 48:10; Jer. 6:27–30; 9:7; Mal. 3:3).

2. Six different instruments are named, two of them wind and the rest string, but the phrase "all kinds of music" (vv. 5, 7) indicates that many more musical instruments were used, and possibly vocal music as well. The wind instruments were the trumpet and the pipes (cornet and flute in KJV), and the string instruments were the five-string lyre (harp), the four-string harp (sackbut), the standard harp (psaltery), and the lute (dulcimer).

3. This raises the question, "Where was Daniel?" He was in charge of

the province in which the ceremony was taking place, and we would expect the king to insist on his presence. Some suggest that Daniel was ill and couldn't attend, so the king excused him. Others believe he had been sent on a special mission by the king and was away from home. A third suggestion is that Daniel, being the ruler of the province, was "behind the scenes," making sure that everything was in order. But surely Daniel wouldn't want to participate in directing such an idolatrous activity. Since the Chaldeans were able to see the three Jewish men refusing to fall down to worship, they must have been on their feet and looking around. This may mean that the king didn't require his advisers to bow down, because he assumed they were loyal to the throne. Hence, if Daniel was absent, he wasn't committing a crime or rebelling against his king.

4. The "number" of this world ruler, the Beast, is 666 (Rev. 13:18), and Nebuchadnezzar's image was sixty cubits high and six cubits wide. Six different musical instruments are also named (Dan. 3:5, 7, 10).

CHAPTER FOUR

1. Verses 28–33 were written by another hand, but Nebuchadnezzar picks up the narrative in verse 34. Daniel himself may have written verses 28–33 and inserted them in the official royal document. Luke followed a similar approach in Acts 23:25–30. Neither the Babylonian king nor the Roman officer was inspired by the Spirit when they wrote, but Daniel and Luke were led by the Spirit to include their writings in what we know as Holy Scripture.

2. Since verses 1–3 were written after the king's recovery, we'll consider them when we study verses 34–37.

3. The Hebrew word translated "flourishing" (v. 4) and "prosperous"

(NIV) means "growing green like a tree" (see Job 15:32; Ps. 92:14; Hos. 14:5). It describes luxurious growth.

4. The word *gods* in verses 9 and 18 is "Elohim" in the original and may be translated "God." But it's not likely that Nebuchadnezzar had the true God of Israel in mind.

5. The KJV translates it "[astonished] for one hour," but the text can be translated "for a moment, for a brief time." It's difficult to believe that the king would wait that long for one of his officers to reply or that the conversation recorded in verse 19 consumed that much time. The NASB reads "appalled for a while."

6. In Isaiah 10:33—11:5, a similar image is used with reference to Messiah. God permitted the "tree" of Israel to be cut down by their enemies, but out from the stump the Messiah would eventually come.

7. In Daniel 5, Belshazzar is called the son of Nebuchadnezzar (vv. 18–22), but it's likely that he was his grandson through his mother who was a daughter of Nebuchadnezzar. In Scripture, the words *son* and *father* are sometimes used in a general sense to mean "relative, descendant."

8. William Culbertson, *The Faith Once Delivered* (Chicago: Moody Press, 1972), 54–55.

9. Did God know that the king would not repent that day? Of course He did, because He knows all things. Did that make His offer less than sincere? No, because neither Daniel nor the king knew what might happen when Daniel urged Nebuchadnezzar to repent. Had the king repented, the Lord would have relented and called off the judgment. The situation was similar to that of Jonah and Nineveh.

10. It's obvious that someone else wrote verses 28–33 since the first person "I" is replaced by the third person "the king." It was likely Daniel who added this to the official report.

11. The phrase "great Babylon" reappears in Revelation 17 and 18, but the city wasn't very great after God finished with it! See also Jeremiah 50—51.

12. While much that's written about werewolves is based on mythology, medical science has recorded the strange mental disease lycanthropy in which the victims think they are animals and they start to look and act like animals. What happened to Nebuchadnezzar was a direct judgment from the Lord that began immediately and ended when Daniel said it would end. This would not be true of a natural affliction.

13. Charles H. Spurgeon, *The New Park Street Pulpit* (Puritan Publications, 1981), vol. 4, 82.

14. A. W. Tozer, *The Knowledge of the Holy* (New York: Harper, 1961), 118.

CHAPTER FIVE

1. At least twenty-three years elapsed between Daniel 4 and Daniel 5, and Daniel 7 and 8 occurred during those years, in the first and third years of Belshazzar's reign (7:1; 8:1). From the king's dream in chapter 2 and the vision in chapter 7, Daniel knew the succession of empires and that the Medes and Persians would conquer the city.

2. The word *father* in vv. 2, 11, 13, 18, and 22 simply means "relative," in this case, his grandfather.

3. The apostrophes represent the letter *aleph,* which is the "soundless" first letter of the Hebrew alphabet. The U in UPHARSIN represents the character for "and."

4. Some scholars think that "Darius" was the title of the Persian ruler just as "Pharaoh" was the title of the Egyptian ruler. This would mean that "Darius the Mede" could have been Cyrus himself.

CHAPTER SIX

1. Daniel 6:28 can be translated, "Even in the reign of Cyrus, the Persian." This would make Darius and Cyrus the same person. However, most translators and Old Testament scholars avoid this approach and see Darius and Cyrus as two different persons.

2. Esther 1:1 and 8:9 state that there were 127 provinces in the Persian kingdom in the reign of Xerxes (486–465). No doubt the political boundaries changed from time to time.

3. In the time of Christ, pious Jews prayed at the third hour (9 a.m.), the ninth hour (3 p.m, the time of the sacrifice at the temple), and at sunset.

4. This question reminds us of the affirmation of faith given by the Daniel's three friends: "Our God whom we serve is able to deliver us" (3:17).

5. The Lord so worked that King Darius obeyed his own law and yet Daniel was still delivered from death. This reminds us that God has worked in a similar way in His great plan of salvation. "The wages of sin is death" (Rom. 6:23), so Jesus Christ died for the sins of the world and paid the debt we cannot pay. But He arose from the dead so that He might forgive all who will receive Him by faith. God obeyed His own law and is therefore "just and the justifier of the one who has faith in Jesus" (Rom. 3:26 NKJV).

6. Daniel's intervention in interpreting Nebuchadnezzar's dream saved the lives of the wise men (Dan. 2:24), and perhaps he would have saved these men and their families also; but it wasn't his decision.

CHAPTER SEVEN

1. During the years between the two world wars, some prophetic students went out on a limb and named Mussolini as the Antichrist and

began counting how many nations allied with Italy. Over the centuries, the chief candidate for Antichrist has been the pope, and each time a new pope is elected, prophecy addicts try to make his name fit in with the number 666 (Rev. 13:18). One man calculated that Napoleon Bonaparte was the Antichrist, but you had to write his name in Arabic and leave out two letters! All sorts of numerical gymnastics have been used to identify "the little horn," but they aren't very convincing.

2. First John 2:18–23 states that "many antichrists" were already in the world at the end of the first century, in the days of the apostle John. These were false teachers who denied the deity and eternal sonship of Jesus Christ. These heretics were not taught by the Holy Spirit but by the spirit of Antichrist, which has its origin in Satan (4:1–4). Satan is a counterfeiter, and his agents, posing as authentic Christian teachers, invaded the churches of the first century and attempted to change the apostolic doctrine (2 Peter 2; Jude).

3. It is possible that the covenant guarantees protection for Israel so they can rebuild their temple in Jerusalem and restore their worship. Of course, Antichrist plans to use the temple for the world to worship him.

4. In the traditional premillennial dispensational interpretation of prophetic Scripture, which is what I have outlined here, the church will be "raptured" and taken to heaven before the final week in Daniel's prophecy occurs (1 Thess. 4:13—5:11). How much time elapses between the rapture of the church and the signing of the covenant hasn't been revealed in Scripture. However, there are those of the dispensational persuasion who believe that the church will be raptured in the middle of the tribulation (Rev. 11:3–19) or at the very end—caught up to be with Christ and then returning with Him in

glory (Rev. 19:11–21). All three schools believe that at His glorious return, Christ will establish a literal kingdom on earth in fulfillment of the Old Testament prophecies.

5. There appears to be no distinction between "the kingdom of God" and "the kingdom of heaven." The Jews were afraid to use God's name lest they be guilty of blasphemy, so they substituted "heaven." Writing especially to the Jews, Matthew uses primarily "kingdom of heaven," while the other writers prefer "kingdom of God."

6. Those who believe that Christ will return before the millennium are called "premillennialists." Those who think that man through the preaching of the gospel will establish the kingdom on earth, and then Christ will return, are called "postmillennialists." Amillennialists are those who do not believe there will be a literal Jewish kingdom on earth, but that the Old Testament's prophecies given to the Jews should be applied spiritually to the church.

7. A. W. Tozer, *I Call It Heresy* (Camp Hill, PA: Christian Publications, 1974), 144–45.

CHAPTER EIGHT

1. Some have suggested that Daniel was in Susa on a diplomatic mission when he received this vision, but Daniel 5:13 indicates that Belshazzar didn't know Daniel and therefore wasn't likely to send him anywhere.

2. "Shepherd" in the Old Testament was the title of a king or royal officer. In the New Testament, it referred to spiritual leaders in the church. The word *pastor* comes from the Latin word for "shepherd."

3. S. Angus in *The Environment of Early Christianity* (London: Duckworth and Co., 1914), 8. In this discussion, I have borrowed a number of helpful thoughts from this excellent book.

4. His name is pronounced "An-TY-i-cus E-PIPH-uh-nees."

CHAPTER NINE

1. The Ahasuerus (Xerxes) named in verse 1 is not the same monarch found in the book of Esther.

2. Note the repetition of the word *great*: a great God (v. 4), the great evil ("disaster," NIV) Israel had brought upon themselves (v. 12), and God's great mercies (v. 18). These three phrases summarize the prayer.

3. Note how often Daniel uses the pronouns "you" and "your" as he refers to the Lord: "your commands ... your people ... your Name ... your truth ... your holy hill." The prayer emphasizes the character of God and not the suffering of the people. This is God-centered praying.

4. The Jewish calendar is based on a series of sevens. The seventh day is the Sabbath day and the seventh year is a sabbatic year (Ex. 23:10–13). The fiftieth year (7 x 7 + 1) is the Year of Jubilee (Lev. 25). The Feast of Pentecost is seven weeks after Firstfruits (Lev. 23:15–22), and during the seventh month of the year, the Jews observed the Feast of Trumpets, the day of Atonement, and the Feast of Tabernacles.

5. If you start with the 457 decree and use lunar years (360 days), you arrive at a similar figure.

6. To make "Messiah, the Prince" (v. 25) and "the prince that shall come" (v. 27) the same person is to confuse Daniel's words. Those who hold to an amillennial interpretation of prophecy take this approach and apply verses 24–27 to the earthly life and ministry of Christ. But His earthly ministry was three years long, not seven years, and the only covenant He established was the New covenant in His blood, a covenant He did not break. While His death on the cross ended the Old Testament economy in the plan of God, the Jewish sacrifices continued for nearly forty years. Jesus did not bring any "abomination of desolation" into the temple; instead, He

sought to purge it of its defilement. It takes a great deal of stretching the text to put it into the past tense.

7. It isn't unusual in Old Testament prophecy for the writer to move his outlook to the end times without warning. In Isaiah 9:6, after the word *given* you move from the birth of Messiah to His kingly reign. Isaiah 61:2 moves suddenly from the gracious ministry of Jesus into the "day of vengeance" (see Luke 4:18–20). Zechariah 9:9 predicts the entrance of Jesus into Jerusalem, but verse 10 moves ahead into the final victory of Christ and His reign of peace.

Chapter Ten

1. This reminds us of the men who were with Saul of Tarsus when he had his vision of Christ. They could hear the Lord's voice but couldn't see the glorious vision that Saul beheld (Acts 9:1–7; 22:9).

2. For the description of another glorious angel, see Revelation 10.

Chapter Eleven

1. It doesn't seem very "scientific" for scholars to assume without proof that their theories are true and the book of Daniel is false. A true scientist considers all the facts impartially and tries to avoid pretrial prejudice. Jesus called Daniel "the prophet" (Matt. 24:15; Mark 13:14), even though nowhere in the book is Daniel called a prophet.

2. This is not the infamous Antiochus Epiphanes whom we met in Daniel 8 and who will appear in 11:21–35.

3. This is not the Cleopatra that Hollywood has glamorized, who lived from 69 to 30 BC. She was mistress to Julius Caesar and later to Mark Antony. She murdered her own brother (who was also her husband) and seized the throne, which she shared with her son Cesarion.

Discovering that Octavianus planned to exhibit her in his "triumph celebration" in Rome, she committed suicide.

CHAPTER TWELVE

1. Some expositors try to fit Antiochus into this section, but they have to twist and turn to do it. In his opposition to everything religious and Jewish, Antichrist will go far beyond anything Antiochus attempted or accomplished. Antiochus wasn't against religion in general, just the Jewish religion. He tried to make his subjects worship the Greek gods and he put a statue of Zeus in the Jewish temple. Antichrist will make himself a god and put his own image in the temple.

2. This outline follows the generally accepted premillennial position and seems to agree with the text.

3. Many students believe that Revelation 6:1–2 describes Antichrist as he begins his rise to power. He has a bow but no arrows; his crown is given to him; and he goes out to conquer. Since he is an "imitation Christ," we expect him to wear a crown and ride a white horse (Rev. 19:11ff.). But Jesus uses the sword of the Word of God, and His crowns are His own.

4. The historic premillennial position teaches that the church will go through the tribulation, be called up when Christ returns, and then come to earth with Him to reign in the kingdom. However, there are those who hold that the church will be raptured before the tribulation (1 Thess. 4:13–18) and will therefore escape the predicted troubles.

5. The Hebrew word is *elohim*, which can mean God or gods. The context determines which you use.

6. Daniel's use of words like *chariots*, *horsemen*, and *ships* doesn't suggest that in the last days nations will revert to ancient methods of warfare. He used words that were meaningful to readers in his day, but we who

read this text today will interpret them in modern terms. The same principle applies to the geographical names in the text, such as Moab, Edom, and Ammon. He is identifying the territories once occupied by those ancient peoples. One argument for making this the battle described in Ezekiel 38—39 is that it occurs at a time when Israel is at peace because of the protection of the man of sin (Ezek. 38:11). Note also that both invasions are like a storm or a whirlwind (Ezek. 38:9; Dan. 11:40).

7. It is the body, not the soul, that sleeps and that is "awakened" at the resurrection. Nowhere does the Bible teach "soul sleep." Death occurs when the spirit leaves the body (James 2:26; Luke 23:46). The spirit of the believer goes immediately to be with the Lord (2 Cor. 5:1–8; Phil. 1:20–24); the spirit of the unbeliever goes to a place of punishment, awaiting the final judgment (Luke 16:19–31). At the last judgment, death will give up the bodies of the unbelievers and hades will give up the spirits (Rev. 20:13).

CHAPTER THIRTEEN

1. A. W. Tozer, *The Set of the Sail* (Christian Publications), 33.
2. D. L. Moody, *Bible Characters* (New York: Fleming H. Revell, 1888), 9.

The "BE" series . . .

For years pastors and lay leaders have embraced Warren W. Wiersbe's very accessible commentary of the Bible through the individual "BE" series. Through the work of David C. Cook Global Mission, the "BE" series is part of a library of books made available to indigenous Christian workers. These are men and women who are called by God to grow the kingdom through their work with the local church worldwide. Here are a few of their remarks as to how Dr. Wiersbe's writings have benefited their ministry.

"Most Christian books I see are priced too high for me . . .
I received a collection that included 12 Wiersbe
commentaries a few months ago and I have
read every one of them.
I use them for my personal devotions every day and they
are incredibly helpful for preparing sermons.
The contribution David C. Cook is making to the
church in India is amazing."

----Pastor E. M. Abraham, Hyderabad, India

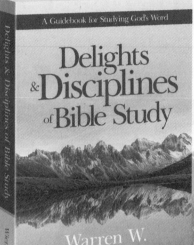